MODERN THEATRE

Modern Theatre

*Extracts from significant plays of
the Nineteenth and Twentieth Centuries*

Compiled and edited by

FRANK PONTON, M.A., Dip. Ed.
(Lecturer in English, Bathurst Teachers' College)

AND

A. W. ASHWORTH, B.A., B. Ec.
(Lecturer in English, Sydney Teachers' College)

THE JACARANDA PRESS

First published 1966 by
JACARANDA PRESS PTY LTD
46 Douglas Street, Milton, Q.
32 Church Street, Ryde, N.S.W.
37 Little Bourke Street, Melbourne, Vic.
142 Colin Street, West Perth, W.A.
154 Marion Road, West Richmond, S.A.
57 France Street, Auckland, N.Z.
P.O. Box 3395, Port Moresby, P.N.G.
122 Regents Park Road, London NW1
70A Greenleaf Road, Singapore 10
P.O. Box 239, Makati, Rizal, Philippines

Reprinted in Hong Kong 1972

© Jacaranda Press Pty Ltd 1966

National Library of Australia
Card Number and ISBN 0 7016 0619 3

CONTENTS

FOREWORD

In this book and an earlier collection, *Classroom Playhouse* 3, the editors have adopted a frankly historical approach to the study of drama. If this approach needs defending, it may be pointed out that the theatre is a dynamic medium of expression, in which a complex of historical circumstances and literary influences are constantly at work. Some knowledge of this complex is needed if any one play is to be properly understood.

It is not intended that this book should replace intensive study of individual plays, but rather augment and assist this study. Under present circumstances in senior schools and colleges, students have some textual knowledge of a few Shakespearian plays and one or two others—perhaps something by Shaw, Wilde, Barrie or Sheridan —but of the rest of dramatic literature they are often entirely ignorant. Obviously, the restricted time available in a crowded syllabus makes this virtually inevitable, but there is no reason why extracts from some of the more significant plays of the Twentieth Century (one of the great ages of drama) should not be brought to students' attention. This book is designed to make this possible and to provide an adequate collection of extracts for private study or class reading.

Many thousands of plays have been written in the last eighty years—so many, in fact, that any collection must be, in part, merely an expression of personal preference. Nevertheless, we have attempted to make our selection representative and to include plays not commonly found elsewhere.

F. P.
A. W. A.

ACKNOWLEDGMENTS

The editors wish to thank the following authors and publishers for permission to print the plays which appear in this selection.

For *Back to Methuselah*: the Public Trustee and the Society of Authors.

For *Tobias and the Angel*: James Bridie, Messrs Curtis Brown Ltd., and the publishers Constable Co.

For *Blithe Spirit*: Noel Coward and the publishers William Heinemann Ltd. The play appeared in *The Collected Plays of Noel Coward*.

For *The Family Reunion*: Faber and Faber Ltd.

For *The Firstborn*: Oxford University Press.

For *Juno and the Paycock*: Sean O'Casey and the publishers Macmillan and Co. Ltd. The play appeared in *Juno and the Paycock and The Plough and the Stars*.

For *Death of a Salesman*: Arthur Miller and Cresset Press. Copyright 1949 by Arthur Miller.

For *The Caucasian Chalk Circle*: Methuen and Co. Ltd. The play appeared in *Plays by Bertolt Brecht*.

For *Ring Round the Moon*: Dr. Jan van Lowen Ltd., Jean Anouilh and Christopher Fry.

For *Maid to Marry*: Eugene Ionesco, Donald Watson and the publishers John Calder Ltd. The play appeared in *Eugene Ionesco: Plays*, Volume III price 10/6 stg.

For *Waiting for Godot*: Samuel Beckett and Faber and Faber Ltd.

INTRODUCTION

During most of the nineteenth century, the standard of drama in England was at an extremely low level. Successful plays of the time had titles like *Sweeney Todd, the Demon Barber of Fleet Street, Maria Marten, or Murder in the Red Barn,* or *Black-Ey'd Susan.* The plots were melodramatic and often absurd, the characterization was utterly devoid of realism, and the writing was unskilful and lacked all literary quality. It is true that successful writers in other fields tried their hands at dramatic writing, but few of their plays were actually performed and, to be fair, it must be admitted that most of them were unplayable. Perhaps the best known of these 'literary' plays is *The Cenci* by the poet Percy Bysshe Shelley. This play has received an occasional performance in recent times, but it is generally considered to be a poor piece in the theatre.

Keeping in mind the rich tradition of English drama, stemming from Shakespeare and continuing into the eighteenth century, it is difficult to account for this apparently sudden decline. Many explanations have been brought forward. It is said, for instance, that the theatre of the eighteenth century had been aristocratic, and that the slowly rising standard of living brought the ordinary people back into the theatre where they demanded something a little more rip-roaring than the comedy of manners and poetic tragedy. Whatever the reason, there is no doubt that cultivated people deserted the straight theatre and turned to novel reading, concert-going and attendance at the opera for relaxation. When considering the nineteenth century, it is easy to call to mind great composers and musicians—Beethoven, Wagner, Chopin, Schubert and Verdi, for example—and great novelists, such as Dickens, Thackeray, the Brontes and Trollope. Until one gets to the end of the century, it is virtually impossible to think of a single playwright of literary merit. No one these days has heard of George Dibdin Pitt, the author of *Sweeney Todd,* or Douglas Jerrold, the author of *Black-Ey'd Susan,* but they were well known men in their day.

The only thing which can be said in their favour is that they attempted to write plays about ordinary people (even if they placed them in extraordinary situations). Gone were the cultivated, leisured characters of Goldsmith and Sheridan, and the Kings and Captains, the Macbeths, the Lears, the Othellos, of Shakespeare. Instead we have the simple country girls, the barbers, the seamen and the Lancashire lads of the typical melodrama. No longer were plays about the love affairs of elegant ladies and gentlemen or about the disasters which could befall great and powerful men; they concerned themselves with murder and robbery and drunkenness among ordinary people.

It is this quality of 'ordinariness' which is the most characteristic thing about the modern drama with which this book deals. We do not mean by this that modern drama is dull; that it certainly is not. But it does not, on the whole, deal with Kings and Heroes and Gods. Its leading characters are salesmen, doctors, novelists, convicts, business men, labourers, ballet dancers, tramps and so on, with the occasional millionaire thrown in for good luck. Even when a playwright invents a superhuman character, like the Angel James Bridie creates in *Tobias and the Angel*, he is very down-to-earth with a somewhat caustic tongue.

But it is obvious that it is not enough just to write plays portraying ordinary people; plays still have to be about something. They have to deal with personal tragedies or social problems, and they have to give an impression of reality. Even a 'highly improbable farce' like Noel Coward's *Blithe Spirit* has something to say about human relationships.

For many years, however, the melodrama held the stage. From 1860 onwards it is true that efforts were made to write plays of greater significance. Playwrights such as T. W. Robertson, Henry Arthur Jones and Sir Arthur Pinero developed a form best described as 'domestic drama', but it was not until about 1880 that a really new kind of play came to be written, and then it appeared not in England, but in Norway. The playwright was Henrik Ibsen, generally regarded as 'the father of modern drama'. Ibsen was already well known, having spent many years writing poetic dramas, the best known of which, *Peer Gynt*, is still played occasionally, but it was not until he began to develop his new ideas that his reputation spread much beyond Scandinavia. The themes of his new plays were social problems of all kinds. In *An Enemy of the*

People, for example, he was concerned with the problem of the naked self-interest of powerful men on the one hand, and the irresponsibility of the democratic majority on the other, and the virtual impossibility for a man of principle to exist when caught between the two. These were plays about ordinary people, but instead of being dull and improbable, they were startling and truthful.

At first they appeared strange and were criticized for their outspoken quality. Slowly, however, they became accepted and were regularly revived, but their appeal was always to a minority of theatregoers. Although they are still frequently performed, Ibsen's plays have seldom been commercially successful in British countries, but their influence has been incalculable. There would be very few modern playwrights who have not been influenced by Ibsen.

One of the men responsible for pointing out the enormous importance of Ibsen's plays was the Irish-born drama critic, George Bernard Shaw. At this time, Shaw was over forty years of age, and although a notable critic, his attempts at writing novels had been failures. He now turned his hand to play-writing and became the most important and the most prolific playwright of the first half of the Twentieth Century. An index of his principal plays alone lists 37 titles, and in spite of the quality being uneven many of these have become some of the best known plays in the language. A random selection of titles follows: *Androcles and the Lion, Arms and the Man* (the basis of the operetta *The Chocolate Soldier*), *Caesar and Cleopatra, Candida, The Devil's Disciple, The Doctor's Dilemma, Heartbreak House, Major Barbara, Man and Superman, The Millionairess, Pygmalion* (the basis of the musical *My Fair Lady*), *Saint Joan* and *Back to Methuselah*.

Shaw's plays may be compared with no others. Professor Allardyce Nicoll, the famous theatre historian, has coined a new phrase to describe them—comedies of purpose. Brilliantly witty, they attempt at the same time to analyse and solve social problems. *Major Barbara*, for example, deals with the problem of poverty and the inadequacy of charity to solve it. But Shaw was a strange mixture of preacher and entertainer and had a rare quality of mind. As a result, there has been no one to follow him, and his plays stand isolated, belonging to no particular 'school' or 'type'.

About 1906, a man who was to become one of the major novelists of the early twentieth century turned his attention to play-writing.

This was John Galsworthy, perhaps known to readers as the author of *The Forsyte Saga*. Galsworthy was a competent, rather than a great, playwright, and his plays are important because they deal with social problems such as legal procedures and strikes in what may be called a 'documentary' fashion. Here was an attempt to portray people as they really are, with little heightening of language, and to use as the basis of the plots happenings as close to actuality as possible.

Ibsen, Shaw and Galsworthy showed the way, but others soon followed. Plays of social comment continued to be written, culminating in about 1938 in *Waiting for Lefty* by the American Clifford Odets. In this play the whole theatre became a Union meeting, and the audience was asked to participate as members of the Union. It was not altogether successful, but it showed the theatre as a forum for discussion.

In the 1890s, when Shaw was beginning his remarkable career, another playwright with great talent, but in a different direction, made his appearance. This was Oscar Wilde, whose *The Importance of Being Earnest*[1] is one of the most delightful comedies in the English language. This play harked back to an earlier time, to the seventeenth and eighteenth centuries, when a type of play known as the 'comedy of manners' flourished. These plays were essentially artificial, and depended for their appeal on witty dialogue and hilarious situations. The characters nearly always came from the leisured upper classes, a tradition which Wilde preserved.

During the course of the twentieth century the comedy of manners underwent a subtle change. Although the characters still had sufficient leisure to get into difficult situations, they shifted down a rung on the social ladder, becoming members of the middle class. A favourite device was to make them novelists, mainly because men following this profession do not have to work from nine till five, but business men and politicians were also introduced. The leading playwrights in this field were Somerset Maugham, the famous novelist and short story writer, and Noel Coward. The comedy of manners has not been much in vogue since the 1930s, but it has a habit of reappearing and may well become popular again.

Another form of comedy which had its roots in the nineteenth century was the 'regional comedy'. In this type of play, full use was made of local idiosyncrasies, both of speech and of manners.

One of the best plays of this type is *When We Are Married* by the Yorkshireman, J. B. Priestley. Priestley calls on his memory of his childhood to draw a hilarious picture of the self-made, north of England business man, intolerant, respectable and uncultivated. Many Irish plays fall partly into this category, but as they often have a serious underlying theme, they will be considered separately.

During the course of the twentieth century, many poets attempted to bring poetry back into the theatre. The example of Shakespeare was before them, and the question was constantly asked: if Shakespeare could write magnificent plays in verse set in his own time, why couldn't we do the same? Many have tried, but success has been limited. One explanation is that the conventions of our theatre are *naturalistic*—that is we use real furniture, attempt to give an impression of a real room, make people eat real food and expect them to smoke real cigarettes—and in such a setting, where everything else appears to be as it is in real life, poetry sits uneasily on the lips of the characters. One of the twentieth century's major poets who has been greatly concerned with this problem is T. S. Eliot. He has written three major plays with modern settings, *The Family Reunion*, *The Cocktail Party* and *The Confidential Clerk*, but has found himself forced to make his verse sound almost like prose to make it acceptable in a modern drawing-room. Without doubt, the most successful verse plays of the century have been set in remote times—two examples being Eliot's own *Murder in the Cathedral* and Christopher Fry's *The Lady's Not For Burning*, both set in the Middle Ages. To illustrate this problem, we have included a scene from *The Family Reunion*, set in a modern drawing-room, and a scene from Fry's *The Firstborn*, set in ancient Egypt.

It should not be forgotten that there were important theatrical movements in other English-speaking countries during the twentieth century—notably in Ireland and America. Ireland had been under English domination for centuries, and had never become reconciled to it in the way the Welsh and the Scots had. For many years before 1914 an Irish nationalist movement had been building up, and the Irish theatre, led by W. B. Yeats, Lady Gregory and J. M. Synge, had been closely allied with it. Taking advantage of England's preoccupation with World War I, the Irish rebels attacked Dublin Post Office during Easter, 1916. The revolt was easily put down, but unrest continued after the war. Eventually, Ireland was partitioned, the southern half becoming the present state of Eire.

A great playwright arose to chronicle these events—Sean O'Casey. Himself from the slums, he caught the remarkably poetic cadence of Irish vernacular speech exactly, and in his plays illustrated the allied elements of farce and tragedy which existed within the Irish situation and within the Irish national character. O'Casey himself continued writing until recently (he died in 1964), and others followed him, notably Paul Vincent Carroll, but no great works have been written since about 1926. It appears that the Irish theatre had done its dash, at least temporarily, once the 'throubles' were over.

No notable work in the theatre appeared in America until after 1920 when a major playwright in Eugene O'Neill came on the scene. Examples of O'Neill's work appear in many anthologies, so he has been omitted from this collection. He was followed by numerous playwrights of the second rank—Clifford Odets, Sidney Kingsley and Maxwell Anderson, among others—but after 1945, two more important figures arose—Tennessee Williams and Arthur Miller. Many of the best plays of these two writers have been made into films and may be familiar to some readers in this form. Both write passionate dramas, often dealing with mental disturbance, and reflect the uneasiness which seems to grip the American soul. The example we have chosen to include is Miller's *Death of a Salesman*, considered by many to be the only genuine tragedy written in the twentieth century.

Meanwhile, in Europe a new renaissance in drama was taking place. In Germany in the twenties Bertolt Brecht came into prominence as a playwright and as a producer, and few plays written today do not show some marks of his influence. In content he belongs with social drama. He felt something was wrong with society and that something should be done about it. Many of his plays are political, but he was too great a dramatist to let this swamp the human content in his best plays. However, rather than the content, it was the techniques and methods of his plays which caught attention and which became a major influence on twentieth century drama. He wrote what was called 'epic theatre'.

This meant that the plays were narratives and the story was very important, as in the old epics. To write his narratives he had to break many of the stage conventions of the time. He wrote in a great number of short scenes which required very little scenery. He used devices like narrators to link them together, screens for film projections, and introduced songs and choruses into the drama. The plays were often interrupted while characters stepped out of their roles to address the audience. He did this, he said, to shake audiences out of their involvement with the human problems he was presenting, so that they might think how they could be solved without violence and tragedy. In effect he was saying: social problems can be solved if we think clearly about them and do not get emotionally involved. His plays are in a sense 'parables of the theatre'.

In France the approach to drama was much more pessimistic. French dramatists like Giraudoux, Anouilh, Sartre and Camus were concerned with the plight of modern man. Unlike Brecht, they wrote in conventional, even classic form. Their plays convey a sense of what they considered the senselessness of life, the devaluation of ideals, beliefs and purposes. Man lived in a dangerous and apparently meaningless world, they felt, but he had freedom of choice and could work out his own destiny if he could come to realize his situation. The plays were often comedies, but bitter comedies or 'black' comedies. The scene we have included from Anouilh's *Ring Round the Moon* shows a millionaire tearing up a fortune in franc notes. It is comedy, but as he is tearing up the symbol of what was his purpose in life, it has a bitter taste. He is beginning to face up to his real position in the world.

A somewhat similar purpose lies behind the 'drama of the absurd', the most strange and startling type of drama produced in this century. It began in France like the 'black' comedies, but its influence spread over the world. In Paris, Ionesco, Adamov, Arrabal and the Irishman, Beckett, all wrote in French their strange and bewildering plays. In America Gelber, Kopit and Albee began to write in this tradition, and in England Pinter, Simpson and others. It is the dramatic 'fashion' of the moment.

The meaning of 'absurd' is not 'ridiculous' as in common usage, but in its dictionary sense of 'out of harmony with reason or propriety; incongruous, unreasonable, illogical'. Man is depicted as absurd in an absurd world, but the point of the drama is that if he can come to realize this he can perhaps do something about it before the world destroys itself.

This type of drama is non-realistic; it abandons all the conventions of character, plot and dialogue which we have become used to in realist drama. The characters are not people in the sense that we expect to see them on the stage, but are often abstracts, types or symbols. In one of Ionesco's plays they turn into rhinoceroses. There is often no plot, merely bewildering happenings, or as in *Waiting for Godot* nothing happens at all. The dialogue is often made of clichés, to show that most of the time when people talk they say nothing at all, and that when they really want to say something important words fail them. Audiences come out from these plays bewildered, and ask: 'What does it mean?' This is what the dramatists want them to ask so that they may begin to think. The plays are comedies with slapstick, farce, rough and tumble, but mostly with strange qualities of menace and tragedy behind them. We have included examples of drama of the absurd from Ionesco and Beckett, two of its leading playwrights. You may be interested to see what you can make of them.

This then is the state of drama in the mid-sixties of this century. It would be wrong, however, to think that drama of the absurd is all that is being written at the moment. In England a strong new revival of realist drama has emerged with the so-called 'kitchen sink' drama. Plays by Arnold Wesker and Shelagh Delaney belong to this. Likewise in Australia realist drama is the characteristic form in plays like Lawler's *Summer of the Seventeenth Doll*, Beynon's *The Shifting Heart* and Seymour's *The One Day of the Year*. The purpose of this book is to show the variety of types of drama that the twentieth century has produced from Ibsen onwards. Nothing like this twentieth century outpouring of drama has occurred since the age of Shakespeare.

[1] See *Classroom Playhouse* 3, pp. 87-99.

The Melodrama of the Nineteenth Century

SWEENEY TODD

The Demon Barber of Fleet Street

(*Act I, Scenes I and II*)

by

George Dibdin Pitt

CHARACTERS

SWEENEY TODD, *The Demon Barber.*
EZEKIAL SMITH, *A mechanic.*
TOBIAS RAGG, *Sweeney Todd's apprentice boy.*
MRS. RAGG, *his mother.*
MARK INGESTRIE, *A mariner.*
JEAN PARMINE, *A lapidary.*

THE AUTHOR

Very little is known of the life of George Dibdin Pitt, except that he wrote a large number of plays which were extremely popular in their time. For a period, in the 1830s, he was stage manager (a position somewhat like that of the modern producer) at the Pavilion Theatre in London, and he died about 1855. Presumably most of his plays were written between these two dates, and it is known that *Sweeney Todd* was first presented in 1842.

THE PLAY

This was the first 'crime play' written in England, and although much of it seems ludicrous to us today, it is no more so, essentially, than many of the films and television programmes produced by Mr. Alfred Hitchcock more recently. In fact, Pitt invented the kind of theatrical entertainment which Hitchcock has made so popular during the last quarter of a century.

The story concerns Sweeney Todd, a villain of the deepest dye, who cut his customers' throats and then, by means of his trick chair, deposited their bodies in his cellar. His method of getting rid of the corpses was ingenious, if revolting. In the cellar they were made into pies by his accomplice in crime, Mrs. Lovett. His profitable business is brought to a halt, however, by the hero of the play, Mark Ingestrie, who survives Sweeney's attack and returns towards the end of the play to obtain his revenge.

Although interesting, *Sweeney Todd* is of no literary value. It is included in this collection as an example of the kind of play which was in vogue a little more than one hundred years ago. It enables us to appreciate the impact made by the plays of Ibsen and Shaw on audiences of the time.

SWEENEY TODD

Scene I

FLEET STREET, LONDON, OUTSIDE SWEENEY TODD'S SHOP.

The shop window is at the back of the stage, the inside of the shop being hidden by a curtain which covers in the back of the window. The window contains a dusty wig on a stand and several bottles. On the curtain, grotesquely enlarged, is the shadow of a barber's chair.
Enter Sweeney Todd, wearing a barber's apron and carrying a razor in his right hand. The razor is usually held behind his back, and occasionally he whets it on the palm of his left hand. With him is Mr. Smith, a mechanic.

TODD: So Mr. Smith—you are come on the matter of that leetle consideration owing to you in respect of your mechanical toy?

SMITH: Yes Mr. Todd, I have brought with me an account for seven pounds eighteen shillings and ninepence ha'penny.

TODD: And what may the ninepence ha'penny be for, Mr. Smith?

SMITH: For one pound of ten inch nails, Mr. Todd.

TODD: And has it occurred to you, Mr. Smith, that some parties might consider ninepence ha'penny a leetle excessive for a pound of ten inch nails?

SMITH: It has occurred to me that I do not like your manner of haggling, Mr. Todd. Do you be pleased to pay me and let me go.

TODD: (*going towards the door of the shop and whetting his razor*) Come a leetle nearer, Mr. Smith. What would you say to a guinea and a half, Mr. Smith? And perhaps a free shave too—afterwards.

SMITH: I would say that you are a rogue, Mr. Todd.

TODD: (*aside*) This individual annoys me. I dislike his method of grabbing money. My gorge rises. I think him mean. With all the pleasure in the world I would shave him—shave him very close. (*To Smith*) I will make it thirty shillings, Mr. Smith. A mere one

3

and sixpence will scarcely embarrass an individual in such a pros-
perous way of business as yourself. Come now, let us say thirty
shillings, Mr. Smith.

SMITH: (*going to Sweeney Todd and speaking very earnestly*) Has
it occurred to you that certain parties not very far up this street—
certain legal parties as you might phrase it—might gain a good
deal of profit and instruction from a perusal of some of the items
and specifications in this little account of mine? Has it occurred
to you that there is what you might call a school a little higher up
this street where a number of individuals keep little bills like this
for their school books? I mean—the Old Bailey, Mr. Todd. (*Aside*)
That will quieten him, I think. (*To Todd*) I think the amount we
mentioned was seven eighteen nine and a half, Mr. Todd.

TODD: I was speaking about a free shave, Mr. Smith. I discern
a roughness about the region of your lower lip and a hairiness about
your throat that makes my razor long to be at it. Pray come in and
take a seat, Mr. Smith . . . . Ha, but here comes Mrs. Ragg. (*Calling
off-stage*) Good morning, Mrs. Ragg. So you have brought the
leetle whelp!

Enter Mrs. Ragg, with her son Tobias. Smith steps aside.

MRS. RAGG: He ain't a little whelp, Mr. Todd, and I won't
have you call him so.

TODD: But only my fun Mrs. Ragg. You know that I dearly
love a jest.

MRS. RAGG: And I axe you to remember that he's very delicate
and not to work him too hard. He comes of a very delicate family
and is easily upset. Aren't you my lamb?

TOBIAS. Yes, please ma.

MRS. RAGG: And I axe you to remember likewise, Mr. Todd,
that my Tobias has been tenderly nurtured and to treat him as
sich. With which I says good morning and leaves you to him,
Mr. Todd.

TODD: Come my young friend.

*Todd seizes Tobias by the wrist and leads him to the door of the
shop. Exit Mrs. Ragg.*

TODD: You will remember now, Tobias Ragg, that you are
my apprentice; that you have had of me board, lodging and washing,
save that you take your meals at home, that you don't sleep here,
and that your mother gets up your linen. (*Fiercely*) Now, are you
not a fortunate, happy dog?

TOBIAS: (*trembling*) Yes sir.

TODD: You will acquire a first-rate profession, quite as good as the law, which your mother tells me that she would have put you to, only that a little weakness of the head-piece unqualified you. And now, Tobias, listen.

TOBIAS: Yes sir.

TODD: I'll cut your throat from ear to ear if you repeat one word of what passes in this shop, or dare to make any supposition, or draw any conclusion from anything you may see or hear, or fancy you see or hear. Do you understand me?

TOBIAS: I won't say anything Mr. Todd.

TODD: Very good. And mark me, the shop, and the shop only, is your place.

TOBIAS: Yes sir.

TODD: And if any customer gives you a penny, you can keep it, so that if you get enough of them you will become a rich man; only I'll take care of them, and when I think you require any—Ay, who's this? His dress and manners bespeak him a seafaring man and a stranger in these parts.

Enter Mark Ingestrie, dressed as a sea captain. He walks round the stage looking about him and examining the names above the shops. Tobias goes up to him. They converse.

TODD: (*to Smith*) I fancy Mr. Mechanic, that I have business with this gentleman. If you will call again some time next week, we may find time to discuss that leetle matter. Thirty shillings, I think, was the sum mentioned between us. In the meantime I dare swear that you have a great deal of business on hand in other parts of the city. I wish you good morning.

SMITH: I will go now, but I will be back before next week, Mr. Todd—considerably before next week.

Smith goes out, and Todd watches Tobias from the shop door.

MARK: (*to Tobias*) I thank you my good boy for the information you have so kindly afforded me. You say that you knew Miss Johanna Oakley?

TOBIAS: Yes sir. I am acquainted with Miss Johanna. She is a kind-hearted lady. Shortly after my father's death, sickness and sorrow overcame my poor mother and myself. Had it not been for Miss Oakley's timely aid, both of us might have perished for want.

MARK: (*aside*) How it gladdens a person's heart to hear his sweetheart so highly esteemed. (*Aloud*) Miss Johanna Oakley is my affianced bride. For five years I have been absent from this country that gave me birth and from the home I love so well. My vessel unexpectedly arrived at this port this morning, and no sooner did I place my foot on shore but I naturally felt a desire to seek out my old friends. Judge of my mortification and surprise when I was told they were not known at their former address, but had removed no one knew whither. Heaven only knows how I should have discovered them, had it not been for the valuable information with which you have supplied me.

TOBIAS: How I should love to become a sailor! Happy and joyous in my freedom, breathing the fresh, pure air of liberty!

MARK: The sea has its perils and its chances. I have been captain of the good ship *Star* for five years. During that time I have saved ten thousand pounds, besides being the possessor of a string of pearls—

There is a chord of villainous music.

TODD: (*aside*) A string of pearls!

MARK: —worth twelve thousand more!

TODD: (*coming down between them*) Ah, Toby my dear—what a time you have been. What has detained you my darling boy?

TOBIAS: (*retreating fearfully*) Sir—Mr. Todd—I—

TODD: Has Captain Pearson's peruke been sent home my dear?

TOBIAS: I—I—I don't know sir.

TODD: (*getting close to Tobias and speaking fiercely*) I thought I gave you instructions never to speak to any person when out of my sight—eh?

TOBIAS: You may have done sir—I—

TODD: (*striking him*) Take that—and remember for the future what it was for. Now go into your shop and attend to your business. The next time you disobey me I'll cut your throat from ear to ear.

MARK: Your pardon sir—I am to blame. I asked him for the address of a particular old friend—we got into conversation—and—

TODD: No apologies, I beg. Boys will be boys, and a little mild chastisement from time to time does them no harm.

MARK: Perhaps you are right, but I must protest always against unnecessary severity towards young persons, who can scarcely be expected to answer for every little fault when hardly capable of judging which is right and wrong. Though hasty, you are no doubt possessed of a generous heart, and hang me if I don't patronize you this very moment. I am going to meet my sweetheart presently, and I think a clean face will become so important an occasion.

TODD: Happy to be of service to you good gentleman. Is it a shave you need? What am I here for but to give you a shave—to give you a closer shave than you have ever had before?

TOBIAS: (*signalling behind Sweeney Todd's back*) You mustn't go in—don't go—don't go!

TODD: (*turning suddenly*) By the way, Tobias, while I am operating on this gentleman's—chin—the figures at St. Dunstan's are about to strike: the exhibition will excite your curiosity and allow me time to shave our customer without interruption.

TOBIAS: Please Mr. Todd, can't I stay and lather him?

TODD: (*fiercely*) Get out, I tell you—get out.

Tobias goes reluctantly.

TODD: I am quite a father to that boy sir. I love him—positively dote on him—so much sir that I feel I could—(*aside*)—polish him off. (*Aloud*) Dear me—I had quite forgotten that you are perhaps in a hurry sir. This way, if you please—pray come in.

Slow music begins. Sweeney stands, bowing at the door. Mark enters the shop. Sweeney pauses for a moment, whetting his razor on the palm of his hand. Then he follows.

Mr. Smith re-enters, finger on lips. He goes to St. Dunstan's churchyard, which is visible at the side of the stage, looks carefully around, then touches a concealed spring on one of the gravestones. It slowly revolves, revealing a secret passage. Mr. Smith begins to descend, then pauses.

SMITH: I have come back Mr. Todd—considerably before next week—

He turns and descends as the curtain falls.

Scene II

INTERIOR OF SWEENEY TODD'S SHOP

There is a window in the centre, with a door on the right. Two pistols hang over the fireplace. Benches, cupboards and stools are ranged round the stage, together with the necessary articles appertaining to the barber's trade. The shaving chair is fixed in the centre of the stage to a revolving trapdoor. Sweeney Todd and Mark Ingestrie are discovered as the curtain rises.

TODD: Will you be pleased to seat yourself? (*He points to the chair.*) Just turn your head a little on one side sir. That will do. (*He brushes Mark's hair.*) You've been to sea, sir?

MARK: Yes: and I have only now lately come up the river from an Indian voyage.

TODD: And you carry some treasures, I presume?

MARK: Among others, this small casket. (*He produces a small casket.*)

TODD: A piece of exquisite workmanship.

MARK: It is not the box but its contents that must cause you wonder, for I must, in confidence, tell you it contains a string of veritable pearls of the value of twelve thousand pounds.

Ominous music begins and continues under the dialogue during the following scene.

TODD: (*chuckling aside, and whetting his razor on his hand*) I shall have to polish him off. Ha, ha, ha! Heugh!

MARK: What the devil noise was that?

TODD: It was only me. I laughed.

MARK: Laugh! Humph! Do you call that a laugh? I suppose you caught it of somebody who died. If that is your way of laughing, I beg you won't do it any more.

TODD: You will find me all attention to your orders good sir. (*He prepares his apparatus for shaving.*) Now sir, we can proceed to business, if it so please you; it's well you came here sir, for though I say it, there isn't a shaving shop in the City of London that ever thinks upon polishing off a customer as I do—fact—can assure you—ha, ha! Heugh!

MARK: Shiver the main brace! I tell you what it is Master Barber: if you come that laugh again I will get up and go. I don't like it, I tell you, and there's an end of it.

TODD: Very good, it won't occur again. (*He mixes up the lather.*) If I may be so bold, who are you? Where did you come from? And whither are you going?

MARK: Humph! That's cool, at all events. Mind, you'll put the brush in my mouth. You seem fond of asking questions my friend; perhaps before I answer them, you will reply to one I'm about to put?

TODD: Oh yes, of course; what is it?

MARK: Do you know a Mr. Oakley, who lives somewhere hereabouts? He is a spectacle maker.

TODD: To be sure I do—Jasper Oakley, in Fore Street. He has a daughter called Johanna, that the young bloods call the flower of Fore Street. Bless me, where can my strop be? I had it this minute—I must have lain it down somewhere. What an odd thing I can't see it; it's very extraordinary what can have become of it. Oh, I recollect—I took it into the parlour. Sit still sir, I shan't be a minute; you can amuse yourself with the newspaper. (*Aside*) I shall soon polish him off!

Sweeney gives Mark the newspaper and goes out. A rushing noise is heard, and Mark, seated on the chair, suddenly disappears from sight, as the trap opens. After a pause, the chair, now empty, reappears as the trap closes. Sweeney Todd enters examining the string of pearls which he holds in his hand. As he stands watching, the chair suddenly disappears and then reappears again.

TODD: What is this? Can I believe my eyes? Some ghostly trick? (*He passes his hand across his brow.*) The chair has life of its own. Terror bedews my forehead. No, no, no—courage Sweeney. It is only that the mechanism is disorganized. And remember— the string of pearls, the string of pearls! When a boy, the thirst of avarice was first awakened by the fair gift of a farthing: that farthing soon became a pound; the pound a hundred—so to a thousand, till I said to myself, I will possess a hundred thousand. This string of pearls will complete the sum. (*He starts.*) Who's there? (*He pounces on Tobias, who has cautiously opened the door.*) Speak—and speak the truth, or your last hour has come! How long were you peeping through the door before you came in?

TOBIAS: Peeping sir?

TODD: Yes, peeping; don't repeat my words, but answer at once; you'll find it better for you in the end.

TOBIAS: Please sir, I wasn't peeping at all.

Sweeney scrutinizes Tobias, and then alters his manner.

TODD: Well, well, if you did peep, what then? It's no matter. I only wanted to know, that's all. It was quite a joke, wasn't it— quite funny, though rather odd, eh? Why don't you laugh, you dog? Come now, there's no harm done, tell me what you thought about, at once; we'll be merry over it—very merry.

TOBIAS: (*puzzled*) Yes, very merry; but I really sir don't know what you mean.

TODD: I mean nothing at all. (*He looks up.*) Who's that at the door.

TOBIAS: It's only the black servant of the gentleman who came here to be shaved this morning.

TODD: Tell the fellow his master is not here; go—let him seek elsewhere, do you hear? (*Aside*) I know I shall have to polish that boy off!

Sweeney whets his razor, while behind his back Tobias discovers the hat worn by Mark. This he secretes.

TOBIAS: (*aside*) 'Tis improbable that he would go without giving notice to his servant. (*Aloud*) Suppose the man won't go?

TODD: (*forgetting himself*) Well then, I shall have to polish him off too.

Tobias goes out. Sweeney looks out of the door.

TODD: If my memory does not deceive me, this should be Jean Parmine, the famous lapidary, the very man I need—fortune is evidently favouring me.

Jean Parmine enters.

PARMINE: Good evening neighbour; I would have you shave me.

TODD: (*as Parmine sits in the chair*) Your servant Mr. Parmine—you deal in precious stones.

PARMINE: Yes I do; but it's rather late for a bargain. Do you want to buy or sell?

TODD: To sell.

PARMINE: Hum! I dare say it's something not in my line, the only order I get is for pearls, and they are not in the market.

TODD: I have nothing but pearls to sell. I mean to keep all my diamonds, garnets and rubies.

PARMINE: The deuce you do! What, do you mean to say you have any of them; be off with you, I'm too old to joke, and am waiting for my supper.

TODD: Will you look at the pearls I have?

PARMINE: Where are they?

TODD: Here! (*He produces the casket and gives it to Parmine.*)

PARMINE: (*examining the pearls*) Real by heaven—all real.

TODD: I know they are real. Will you deal with me or not?

PARMINE: I'm not quite sure that they are real; let me look at them again. Oh, I see, counterfeit; but so well done that really for the curiosity of the thing I will give you fifty pounds.

TODD: Fifty pounds? Who is joking now I wonder? We cannot deal tonight.

PARMINE: Stay—I will give you a hundred.

TODD: Hark ye friend, it neither suits my inclination or my time to stand haggling with you. I know the value of pearls, and as a matter of ordinary business I will sell them to you so that you may get a handsome profit.

PARMINE: Well, since you know more than I gave you credit for, and this is to be a downright business transaction, I think I can find a customer who will pay £11,000 for them; if so, I have no objection to advance the sum of £8,000.

TODD: I am content—let me have the money early tomorrow.

PARMINE: Stop a bit; there are some rather important things to consider—you must know that a string of pearls is not to be bought like a few ounces of old silver, and the vendor must give every satisfaction as to how he came by them.

TODD: (*aside*) I am afraid I shall have to polish him off. (*Aloud*) Psha man, who will question you, who are known to be in the trade?

PARMINE: That's all very fine; but I don't see why I should give you the full value of an article without evidence to prove your title to it.

TODD: Or in other words, you don't care how I possess the property provided I sell it to you at a thief's price; but if, on the contrary, I want their real value, you mean to be particular.

PARMINE: I suspect you have no right to dispose of the pearls, and to satisfy myself I shall insist on your accompanying me to a magistrate.

TODD: And what road shall you take?

PARMINE: The right road!

TODD: (*who has edged towards the door, springs into the next room and shouts from offstage*) Then off you go Mr. Parmine; good-bye, good-bye, good-bye!

Parmine and the chair disappear from sight and Todd breaks into demoniacal laughter. Smith enters from a secret door.

SMITH: Not at all Mr. Todd; not good-bye, but how d'ye do, *dear* Mr. Todd!

TODD: (*standing aghast and then speaking slowly*) So you know that secret too. It is enough. Your bill is paid.

SMITH: But it has to be receipted yet Mr. Todd.

TODD: And it was you too that was responsible for the sudden liveliness of my chair just now, eh? You are a leetle too clever Mr. Smith. I do not like to have such a clever mechanic in my confidence. It does not altogether suit.

Sweeney draws a pistol quickly from his breast and fires. Smith falls. Sweeney lifts the body into the chair.

TODD: Ha! Mr. Clever Smith—you won't do much thinking now, I suppose, with that bleeding head. You can take all your cleverness down below now; you can have a little ride in this very particular chair of yours—it ought to work well now its master is sitting in it.

Smith and the chair disappear from sight and the curtain falls as Sweeney breaks into further peals of demoniacal laughter.

Plays of Social Comment

AN ENEMY OF THE PEOPLE

(Act II)
by
Henrik Ibsen
(Based on the William Archer version, translated by
Eleanor Marx-Aveling.)

CHARACTERS

DR. THOMAS STOCKMANN, *Medical Officer to the Town Baths.*
MRS. STOCKMANN, *his wife.*
PETRA, *their daughter, a teacher.*
EILEF, MORTEN, *their schoolboy sons.*
PETER STOCKMANN, *The doctor's eldest brother, Burgomaster and Chief of Police, Chairman of the Baths Committee, etc.*
MORTEN KIIL, *Mrs. Stockmann's adopted father, a master tanner.*
HOVSTAD, *Editor of* The Poeple's Messenger.
ASLAKSEN, *a printer.*

THE AUTHOR

Henrik Ibsen was born in Norway in 1828 and died in 1906. He first became known as a poetic dramatist, but in the later period of his life began to write the prose plays for which he has become famous.

One of England's leading dramatic critics, William Archer, who was himself part Norwegian, was mainly responsible for getting most of Ibsen's plays translated into English, and it is his version of *An Enemy of the People* which is used here.

THE PLAY

An Enemy of the People deals with the efforts of an idealistic doctor, Thomas Stockmann, to get the Town Council to take action to remove a public health hazard. He has discovered that the Town Baths are polluted, but as these Baths and the town's reputation as a health resort are the main reasons for visitors coming in the summer months, he soon finds great opposition to his plans to remedy the situation. His main opponent is his own brother who is Burgomaster or Mayor. At first he receives some support, particularly from the editor of a local paper and the leader of the Ratepayers' Association, but when they discover that Stockmann's improvements will be very costly and that the publicity may ruin the town's reputation as a health resort, they turn against him. Finally, there is a public meeting which Stockmann attends, fully convinced that the people will support him. Again he is disappointed. He is declared 'an enemy of the people', and he learns the bitter truth that people tend to believe only what they want to believe—particularly where their pockets are concerned. If he wishes to proclaim the truth, he must stand alone, reviled and ridiculed by the men in power and by the ordinary people.

An Enemy of the People deals with the ordinary, everyday world, whereas plays like *Sweeney Todd* are concerned with a strange world of fantasy and nightmare. Ibsen's purpose is to lay bare

the drama of real life, and to explore the behaviour of individuals and communities faced with difficult situations. In this play, he finds that neither powerful men nor 'compact democratic majorities' are much concerned with truth and principle when their own interests are threatened. It is not a hopeful play, and it provides no easy answer to grave social problems. Ibsen, however, wished to bring these matters out into the open, and he was the first playwright in modern times to do this successfully.

AN ENEMY OF THE PEOPLE

Act II

The scene is Dr. Stockmann's sitting-room; simply but neatly decorated and furnished. In the wall to the right are two doors, the further one leading to the hall, the nearer one to the doctor's study. In the opposite wall, facing the hall door, there is a door leading to the other rooms of the house. Against the middle of this wall stands the stove; further forward a sofa with a mirror above it, and in front of it an oval table with a cover. On the table is a lamp, with a shade. In the back wall there is a door leading to the dining room, but at the moment this is closed.

It is morning in a small town on the South Coast of Norway, about the year 1882.

Mrs. Stockmann enters from the dining room with a sealed letter in her hand, goes to the foremost door on the right, and peeps in.

MRS. STOCKMANN: Are you there, Thomas?

STOCKMANN: (*within*) Yes, I have just come in. (*He enters.*) What is it?

MRS. STOCKMANN: A letter from your brother. (*She hands it to him.*)

STOCKMANN: Aha, let us see. (*He opens the envelope and reads.*) 'The MS, sent me, is returned herewith—' (*He reads on, mumbling to himself.*) H'm—

MRS. STOCKMANN: Well, what does he say?

STOCKMANN: (*putting the paper in his pocket*) Nothing; only that he'll come up himself about midday.

MRS. STOCKMANN: Then be sure you remember to stay at home.

STOCKMANN: Oh, I can easily manage that; I've finished my morning's visits.

MRS. STOCKMANN: I am very curious to know how he takes it.

STOCKMANN: You'll see he won't be over-pleased that I am the one who made the discovery, and not himself.

MRS. STOCKMANN: Ah, that's just what I'm afraid of.

STOCKMANN: Of course at bottom he'll be glad. But still—

16

Peter is damnably unwilling that anyone but himself should do anything for the good of the town.

MRS. STOCKMANN: Do you know, Thomas, I think you might stretch a point, and share the honour with him. Couldn't it appear that he put you on the track—?

STOCKMANN: By all means, for all I care. If only I can get things put straight—

Old Morten Kiil puts his head in at the hall door.

KIIL: (*slyly*) Is it—is it true?

MRS. STOCKMANN: (*going towards him*) Father—is that you?

STOCKMANN: Hallo, father-in-law! Good morning, good morning.

MRS. STOCKMANN: Do come in.

KIIL: Yes, if it's true; if not, I'm off again.

STOCKMANN: If what is true?

KIIL: This crazy business about the water-works. Now, is it true?

STOCKMANN: Why, of course it is. But how did you come to hear of it?

KIIL: (*coming in*) Petra looked in on her way to the school—

STOCKMANN: Oh, did she?

KIIL: Ay, ay—and she told me—I thought she was only making game of me; but that's not like Petra either.

STOCKMANN: No indeed; how could you think so?

KIIL: Oh, you can never be sure of anybody. You may be made a fool of before you know where you are. So it is true, after all?

STOCKMANN: Most certainly it is. Do sit down, father-in-law. (*He forces him down on the sofa.*) Now isn't it a real blessing for the town?

KIIL: (*suppressing his laughter*) A blessing for the town?

STOCKMANN: Yes, that I made the discovery in time.

KIIL: Ay, ay, ay! Well, I could never have believed that you would play monkey-tricks with your very own brother.

STOCKMANN: Monkey-tricks!

MRS. STOCKMANN: Why, father dear—

KIIL: (*resting his hand and chin on the top of his stick, and blinking slyly at the doctor*) What was it again? Wasn't it that some animals had got into the water-pipes?

STOCKMANN: Yes; infusorial animals.

KIIL: And any number of these animals had got in, Petra said— whole swarms of them.

STOCKMANN: Certainly; hundreds of thousands.

KIIL: But no one can see them—isn't that it?

STOCKMANN: Quite right; no one can see them.

KIIL: (*with a quiet, chuckling laugh*) I'll be damned if that isn't the best thing I've heard of you yet.

STOCKMANN: What do you mean?

KIIL: But you'll never in this world make the Burgomaster take in anything of the sort.

STOCKMANN: Well, we shall see.

KIIL: Do you really think he'll be so crazy?

STOCKMANN: I hope the whole town will be so crazy.

KIIL: The whole town! Well, I don't say it won't. But it serves them right; it'll teach them a lesson. They wanted to be so much cleverer than we old fellows. They hounded me out of the Town Council. Yes; I tell you they hounded me out like a dog, that they did. But now it's their turn. Just you keep up the game with them, Stockmann.

STOCKMANN: Yes, but father-in-law—

KIIL: Keep it up, I say. (*He rises.*) If you can make the Burgomaster and his gang eat humble pie, I'll give a hundred crowns straight away to the poor.

STOCKMANN: Come, that's good of you.

KIIL: Of course I've little enough to throw away; but if you can manage that, I'll certainly remember the poor at Christmas-time, to the tune of fifty crowns.

Hovstad enters from the hall.

HOVSTAD: Good morning! (*He pauses as he sees Kiil.*) Oh! I beg your pardon—

STOCKMANN: Not at all. Come in, come in.

KIIL: (*chuckling again*) He! Is he in it too?

HOVSTAD: What do you mean?

STOCKMANN: Yes, of course he is.

KIIL: I might have known it! It's to go into the papers. Ah, you're the one, Stockmann! You lay your heads together; I'm off.

STOCKMANN: Oh no; don't go yet, father-in-law.

KIIL: No, I'm off now. Play them all the monkey-tricks you can think of. Deuce take me, but you shan't lose by it. (*He goes out, accompanied by Mrs. Stockmann.*)

STOCKMANN: (*laughing*) What do you think—? The old fellow doesn't believe a word of all this about the water-works.

HOVSTAD: Was that what he—?

STOCKMANN: Yes, that was what we were talking about. And I daresay you have come on the same business?

HOVSTAD: Yes. Have you a moment to spare, doctor?

STOCKMANN: As many as you like, my dear fellow.

HOVSTAD: Have you heard anything from the Burgomaster?

STOCKMANN: Not yet. He'll be here presently.

HOVSTAD: I have been thinking the matter over since last evening.

STOCKMANN: Well?

HOVSTAD: To you, as a doctor and a man of science, this business of the water-works appears an isolated affair. I daresay it hasn't occurred to you that a good many other things are bound up with it?

STOCKMANN: Indeed! In what way? Let us sit down, my dear fellow—No; there, on the sofa.

Hovstad sits on the sofa: the doctor in an easy chair on the other side of the table.

STOCKMANN: Well, so you think—?

HOVSTAD: You said yesterday that the water is polluted by impurities in the soil.

STOCKMANN: Yes, undoubtedly; the mischief comes from that poisonous swamp up in the Mill Dale.

HOVSTAD: Excuse me, doctor, but I think it comes from a very different swamp.

STOCKMANN: What swamp may that be?

HOVSTAD: The swamp in which our whole municipal life is rotting.

STOCKMANN: The devil, Mr. Hovstad! What notion is this you've got hold of?

HOVSTAD: All the affairs of the town have gradually drifted into the hands of a pack of bureaucrats—

STOCKMANN: Come now, they're not all bureaucrats.

HOVSTAD: No; but those who are not are the friends and adherents of those who are. We are entirely under the thumb of a ring of wealthy men, men of old family and position in the town.

STOCKMANN: Yes, but they are also men of ability and insight.

HOVSTAD: Did they show ability and insight when they laid the water-pipes where they are?

STOCKMANN: No; that, of course, was a piece of stupidity. But that will be set right now.

HOVSTAD: Do you think it will go so smoothly?

STOCKMANN: Well, smoothly or not, it will have to be done.

HOVSTAD: Yes, if the press exerts its influence.

STOCKMANN: Not at all necessary, my dear fellow; I'm sure my brother—

HOVSTAD: Excuse me, doctor, but I must tell you that I am thinking of taking the matter up.

STOCKMANN: In the paper?

HOVSTAD: Yes. When I took over *The People's Messenger*, I was determined to break up the ring of obstinate old blockheads who held everything in their hands.

STOCKMANN: But you told me yourself what came of it. You nearly ruined the paper.

HOVSTAD: Yes, at that time we had to draw in our horns, that's true enough. The whole Bath scheme might have fallen through if these men had been sent about their business. But now the Baths are an accomplished fact, and we can get on without these august personages.

STOCKMANN: Get on without them, yes; but we still owe them a great deal.

HOVSTAD: The debt shall be duly acknowledged. But a journalist of my democratic tendencies cannot let such an opportunity slip through his fingers. We must explode the tradition of official infallibility. That rubbish must be got rid of, like every other superstition.

STOCKMANN: There I am with you with all my heart, Mr. Hovstad. If it's a superstition, away with it!

HOVSTAD: I should be sorry to attack the Burgomaster, as he is your brother. But I know you think with me—the truth before all other considerations.

STOCKMANN: Why, of course. (*Vehemently.*) But still—! But still—!

HOVSTAD: You mustn't think ill of me. I am neither more self-interested nor more ambitious than other men.

STOCKMANN: Why, my dear fellow—who says you are?

HOVSTAD: I come of humble folk, as you know; and I have had ample opportunities of seeing what the lower classes really require. And that is to have a share in the direction of public affairs, doctor. That is what develops ability and knowledge and self-respect—

STOCKMANN: I understand that perfectly.

HOVSTAD: Yes; and I think a journalist incurs a heavy responsibility if he lets slip a chance of helping to emancipate the downtrodden masses. I know well enough that our oligarchy will denounce me as an agitator, and so forth; but what do I care? If only my conscience is clear, I—

STOCKMANN: Just so, just so, my dear Mr. Hovstad. But still —deuce take it—! (*There is a knock at the door.*) Come in!

Aslaksen, the printer, appears at the door leading to the hall. He is humbly but respectably dressed in black, wears a white necktie, slightly crumpled, and has a silk hat and gloves in his hand.

ASLAKSEN: (*bowing*) I beg pardon, doctor, for making so bold—

STOCKMANN: (*rising*) Hallo! If it isn't Mr. Aslaksen!

ASLAKSEN: Yes, it's me, doctor.

HOVSTAD: (*rising*) Is it me you want, Aslaksen?

ASLAKSEN: No, not at all. I didn't know you were here. No, it's the doctor himself—

STOCKMANN: Well, what can I do for you?

ASLAKSEN: Is it true, what Mr. Billing tells me, that you're going to get us a better set of water-works?

STOCKMANN: Yes, for the Baths.

ASLAKSEN: Of course, of course. Then I just looked in to say that I'll back up the movement with all my might.

HOVSTAD: (*to the doctor*) You see!

STOCKMANN: I'm sure I thank you heartily; but—!

ASLAKSEN: You may find it not such a bad thing to have us small middle-class men at your back. We form what you may call a compact majority in the town—when we really make up our minds, that's to say. And it's always as well to have the majority with you, doctor.

STOCKMANN: No doubt, no doubt; but I can't conceive that any special measures will be necessary in this case. I should think that in so clear and straightforward a matter—

ASLAKSEN: Yes, but all the same, it can do no harm. I know the local authorities very well—the powers that be are not over-ready to adopt suggestions from outsiders. So I think it wouldn't be amiss if we made some sort of a demonstration.

HOVSTAD: Precisely my opinion.

STOCKMANN: A demonstration, you say? But in what way would you demonstrate?

ASLAKSEN: Of course with great moderation, doctor. I always insist upon moderation; for moderation is a citizen's first duty—at least that's my way of thinking.

STOCKMANN: We all know that, Mr. Aslaksen.

ASLAKSEN: Yes, I think my moderation is generally recognized. And this affair of the water-works is very important for us small middle-class men. The Baths bid fair to become, as you might say, a little gold-mine for the town. We shall all have to live by the Baths, especially we house-owners. So we want to support the Baths all we can; and as I am Chairman of the House-owners' Association—

STOCKMANN: Well—?

ASLAKSEN: And as I am an active worker for the Temperance Society—of course you know, doctor, that I'm a temperance man?

STOCKMANN: To be sure, to be sure.

ASLAKSEN: Well, you'll understand that I come in contact with a great many people. And as I'm known to be a prudent and law-abiding citizen, as you yourself remarked, doctor, I have a certain influence in the town, and hold some power in my hands—though I say it that shouldn't.

STOCKMANN: I know that very well, Mr. ᴧslaksen.

ASLAKSEN: Well then, you see—it would be easy for me to get up an address, if it came to a pinch.

STOCKMANN: An address?

ASLAKSEN: Yes, a kind of note of thanks to you, from the citizens of the town, for your action in a matter of such general concern. Of course it will have to be drawn up with all fitting moderation, so as to give no offence to the authorities and parties in power. But so long as we're careful about that, no one can take offence, I should think.

HOVSTAD: Well, even if they didn't particularly like it—

ASLAKSEN: No no no; no offence to the powers that be, Mr. Hovstad. No opposition to people that can take it out of us again so easily. I've had enough of that in my time; no good ever comes of it. But no one can object to the free but temperate expression of a citizen's opinion.

STOCKMANN: (*shaking his hand*) I can't tell you, my dear Mr. Aslaksen, how heartily it delights me to find so much support among my fellow townsmen. I'm so happy—so happy! Come, you'll have a glass of sherry? Eh?

ASLAKSEN: No, thank you; I never touch spirituous liquors.

STOCKMANN: Well then, a glass of beer—what do you say to that?

ASLAKSEN: Thanks, not that either, doctor. I never take anything so early in the day. And now I'll be off round the town, and talk to some of the house-owners, and prepare public opinion.

STOCKMANN: It's extremely kind of you, Mr. Aslaksen; but I really can't get it into my head that all these preparations are necessary. The affair seems to me so simple and self-evident.

ASLAKSEN: The authorities always move slowly, doctor—God forbid I should blame them for it—

HOVSTAD: We'll stir them up in the paper tomorrow, Aslaksen.

ASLAKSEN: No violence, Mr. Hovstad. Proceed with moderation, or you'll do nothing with them. Take my advice; I've picked up experience in the school of life. And now I'll say good morning, doctor. You know that at least you have us small middle-class men behind you, solid as a wall. You have the compact majority on your side, doctor.

STOCKMANN: Many thanks, my dear Mr. Aslaksen. (*He holds out his hand.*) Good-bye, good-bye.

ASLAKSEN: Are you coming to the office, Mr. Hovstad?

HOVSTAD: I shall come presently. I have still one or two things to arrange.

ASLAKSEN: Very well. (*He bows and goes out to the hall. Dr. Stockmann accompanies him.*)

HOVSTAD: (*as the doctor re-enters*) Well, what do you say to that, doctor? Don't you think it is high time we gave this half-hearted cowardice a good shaking up?

STOCKMANN: Are you referring to Aslaksen?

HOVSTAD: Yes, I am. He's a decent enough fellow, but he's one of those sunk in the swamp. And most people here are just like him; they are always wavering and wobbling from side to side; what with scruples and misgivings, they never dare advance a step.

STOCKMANN: Yes, but Aslaksen seems to me thoroughly well-intentioned.

HOVSTAD: There is one thing I value more than good intentions, and that is an attitude of manly self-reliance.

STOCKMANN: There I am quite with you.

HOVSTAD: So I am going to seize this opportunity, and see if I can't for once put a little grit into their good intentions. The worship of authority must be rooted up in this town. This gross, inexcusable blunder of the water-works must be brought home clearly to every voter.

STOCKMANN: Very well. If you think it's for the good of the community, so be it; but not till I have spoken to my brother.

HOVSTAD: At all events, I shall be writing my leader in the meantime. And if the Burgomaster won't take the matter up—

STOCKMANN: But how can you conceive his refusing?

HOVSTAD: Oh, it's not inconceivable. And then—

STOCKMANN: Well then, I promise you—Look here, in that case you may print my paper—put it in just as it is.

HOVSTAD: May I? Is that a promise?

STOCKMANN: (*handing him the manuscript*) There it is; take it with you. You may as well read it in any case; you can return it to me afterwards.

HOVSTAD: Very good; I shall do so. And now, good-bye, doctor.

STOCKMANN: Good-bye, good-bye. You'll see it will all go smoothly, Mr. Hovstad—as smoothly as possible.

HOVSTAD: Hmm—we shall see. (*He bows and goes out through the hall.*)

STOCKMANN: (*going to the dining-room door and looking in*) Katrina! Hallo! Are you back, Petra?

PETRA: (*entering*) Yes, I've just got back from school.

MRS. STOCKMANN: (*entering*) Hasn't he been here yet?

STOCKMANN: Peter? No; but I have been having a long talk with Hovstad. He's quite enthusiastic about my discovery. It turns out to be of much wider importance than I thought at first. So he has placed his paper at my disposal, if I should require it.

MRS. STOCKMANN: Do you think you will?

STOCKMANN: No. But at the same time, I feel proud to know that the enlightened, independent press is on my side. And what do you think—I have had a visit from the Chairman of the House-owners' Association too.

MRS. STOCKMANN: Really? What did he want?

STOCKMANN: To assure me of his support. They will all stand by me at a pinch. Katrina, do you know what I have behind me?

MRS. STOCKMANN: Behind you? No. What have you behind you?

STOCKMANN: The compact majority!

MRS. STOCKMANN: Oh! Is that good for you, Thomas?

STOCKMANN: Yes indeed; I should think it was good. (*He rubs his hands as he walks up and down.*) Good God! Isn't it a delight to feel so close to one's fellow townsmen?

PETRA: And to do so much that's good and useful, father!

STOCKMANN: And all for the sake of one's native town!

A bell rings.

MRS. STOCKMANN: There's the bell.

STOCKMANN: It must be the Burgomaster. (*There is a knock at the hall door.*) Come in!

Burgomaster Stockmann enters from the hall.

BURGOMASTER: Good morning.

STOCKMANN: I'm glad to see you, Peter.

MRS. STOCKMANN: Good morning, brother-in-law. How are you?

BURGOMASTER: Well enough, thank you. (*To the doctor.*) Yesterday evening, after office hours, I received from you a dissertation upon the state of the water in the Baths.

STOCKMANN: Yes. Have you read it?

BURGOMASTER: I have.

STOCKMANN: And what do you think of it?

BURGOMASTER: (*with a sidelong look at the two women*) Well—

MRS. STOCKMANN: Come, Petra.

Mrs. Stockmann and Petra go into the room on the left.

BURGOMASTER: (*after a pause*) Was it necessary to make all these investigations behind my back?

STOCKMANN: Yes, till I was absolutely certain, I–

BURGOMASTER: And you are absolutely certain now?

STOCKMANN: My paper must surely have convinced you of that.

BURGOMASTER: Is it your intention to submit this statement to the Board of Directors, as a sort of official document?

STOCKMANN: Of course. Something must be done in the matter, and as soon as possible.

BURGOMASTER: In your usual fashion, you make very strong statements in your report. Amongst other things, you say that what we offer our visitors is not healthful, but a slow poison.

STOCKMANN: Why, Peter, what else can it be called? Just think of it—poisoned water which is used both internally and externally! And by poor invalids who come to us in all conditions, and pay us handsomely to cure them!

BURGOMASTER: And then you announce as your conclusion that we must build a sewer to carry off the alleged impurities from the Mill Dale, and must re-lay all the water pipes.

STOCKMANN: Yes. Can you suggest any other plan? I can't think of one.

BURGOMASTER: I found a pretext for looking in on the Town Engineer this morning, and—in a half-jesting way—I mentioned these alterations as things we might possibly have to consider, at some future time.

STOCKMANN: At some future time!

BURGOMASTER: Of course he smiled at what he thought my extravagance. Have you taken the trouble to think what your proposed alterations would cost? From what the engineer said, I gathered that it would probably be several hundred thousand crowns.

STOCKMANN: As much as that?

BURGOMASTER: But that is not the worst. The work would take at least two years.

STOCKMANN: Two years! Do you mean to say two whole years?

BURGOMASTER: At least. And what are we to do with the Baths in the meantime? Are we to close them? Do you think anyone would come here, if the news got around that the water was contaminated?

STOCKMANN: But, Peter, that's precisely what it is.

BURGOMASTER: This would have to happen just when the Baths are doing so well. Neighbouring towns, too, can claim to be health resorts, and don't you think they would at once attempt to divert the stream of visitors to themselves? Of course they would; and we should be left stranded. We should probably have to give up the whole undertaking; so you would have ruined your native town.

STOCKMANN: I—ruined—

BURGOMASTER: The Baths give the town any future worth speaking of, and they're the only thing that does. You must know that as well as I do.

STOCKMANN: Then what do you think should be done?

BURGOMASTER: I have not succeeded in convincing myself that the condition of the water in the Baths is as bad as you make it out to be.

STOCKMANN: I tell you, if it's anything it's worse—or will be in the summer, when the hot weather sets in.

BURGOMASTER: I repeat that I believe you exaggerate greatly. A competent physician should know what measures to take—he should be able to remove harmful substances, or at least make them less noticeable if they should make their presence felt.

STOCKMANN: Indeed—? And then—?

BURGOMASTER: The existing water-works are, once and for all, a fact, and must be treated as such. But when the time comes, the Directors will probably consider whether it may not be possible, without unreasonable financial sacrifices, to make certain improvements.

STOCKMANN: And do you imagine I could ever be a party to such dishonesty?

BURGOMASTER: Dishonesty?

STOCKMANN: Yes, dishonesty—a fraud, a lie, an absolute crime against the public, against society as a whole!

BURGOMASTER: As I remarked before, I have not been able to convince myself that there is really any immediate danger.

STOCKMANN: You have! You must have! I know that my report is absolutely clear and convincing. And you understand it perfectly, Peter, only you won't admit it. It was you who insisted that both the Baths and the water-works should be placed where they are now; and it's that—it's that damned blunder that you won't confess. Do you think I don't see through you?

BURGOMASTER: And even if you are right, why do you think I do it? For the good of the town. Without moral authority I cannot guide and direct affairs in the way I consider conducive to the general welfare. Because of this—and for other reasons as well—it is most important to me that your report should not be submitted to the Board of Directors. It must be kept back, for the good of the community. Later on, I will bring the matter up for discussion, and we will do the best we can, quietly; but not a word, not a whisper, of this unfortunate business must come to the public ears.

STOCKMANN: But it can't be prevented now, my dear Peter.

BURGOMASTER: It must and shall be prevented.

STOCKMANN: It can't be, I tell you; far too many people know about it already.

BURGOMASTER: Know about it! Who? Surely not those fellows on *The People's Messenger*—?

STOCKMANN: Oh yes; they know. The liberal, independent press will take care that you do your duty.

BURGOMASTER: (*after a pause*) You are an amazingly reckless man, Thomas. Haven't you thought how this may affect yourself?

STOCKMANN: Affect me?

BURGOMASTER: Yes—and your family.

STOCKMANN: What the devil do you mean?

BURGOMASTER: I believe I have always shown myself ready and willing to lend you a helping hand.

STOCKMANN: Yes, you have, and I thank you for it.

BURGOMASTER: I ask no thanks. In fact I was, to some extent, forced to act as I did. I hoped that I should be able to keep you a little in check if I helped to improve your financial position.

STOCKMANN: What! So it was only for your sake—!

BURGOMASTER: To some extent, as I said. It is difficult for a man in an official position when his nearest relative goes and compromises himself, time after time.

STOCKMANN: And you think I do that?

BURGOMASTER: Yes, unfortunately you do, without knowing it. You have a turbulent, unruly, rebellious spirit. And then you have an unhappy propensity for rushing into print upon every possible and impossible occasion. You no sooner hit on an idea, than you have to write an article or a whole pamphlet about it.

STOCKMANN: Isn't it a citizen's duty, when he has conceived a new idea, to communicate it to the public?

BURGOMASTER: Oh, the public doesn't need any new ideas. It gets on best with the good old ones it has already.

STOCKMANN: You say that to my face!

BURGOMASTER: Yes, I must speak frankly to you for once. Before this, I have tried to avoid it, for I know how irritable you are; but now I must tell you the truth, Thomas. You have no idea how much you injure yourself by your officiousness. You complain of the authorities, and of the government itself; you cry them down and maintain that you have been slighted and persecuted. But what else can you expect, with your impossible disposition?

STOCKMANN: Oh, indeed! I'm impossible, am I?

BURGOMASTER: Yes, Thomas, you are an impossible man to work with. I know that from experience. You have no consideration for anyone or anything; you seem to forget that you have me to thank for your position as Medical Officer to the Baths.

STOCKMANN: It was mine by right! Mine and no one else's! I was the first to discover the town's possibilities as a watering-place; I saw them, and at that time I was the only one who did. For years I fought single-handed; I wrote and wrote—

BURGOMASTER: No doubt; but the time wasn't ripe. Of course, in that out-of-the-world corner where you were at the time, you couldn't see that. As soon as the right moment arrived, I—and others—took the matter in hand.

STOCKMANN: Yes, and you went and bungled the whole of my wonderful plan. We can see now what a set of wiseacres you were!

BURGOMASTER: All I can see is that you are again looking for an outlet for your pugnacity. You want to attack your superiors—that's an old habit of yours. You can't endure any authority over you; you look sideways at anyone who holds a higher post than you do; you regard him as a personal enemy—and don't care what kind of weapon you use against him. But now I have shown you how much is at stake for the town and consequently for me as well. And I warn you, Thomas, that I am inexorable in the demand I am about to make of you.

STOCKMANN: What demand?

BURGOMASTER: You have not had the sense to refrain from chattering to outsiders about this delicate business, which should have been kept an official secret, so it cannot now be hushed up. All sorts of rumours will get around, and those not well-disposed will invent all kinds of additions to them. Therefore it will be necessary for you to contradict these rumours publicly.

STOCKMANN: I contradict—! I don't understand you.

BURGOMASTER: We expect that, after further investigation, you will come to the conclusion that the affair is not nearly so serious or pressing as you had at first imagined.

STOCKMANN: Aha! So you expect that?

BURGOMASTER: Furthermore, we expect you to express your confidence that the Board of Directors will conscientiously carry out any necessary measures to remedy any possible defects.

STOCKMANN: Yes, but you'll never be able to do it, as long as you go on tinkering and patching. I tell you that, Peter, and it's my sincere and deepest conviction—

BURGOMASTER: As an official, you have no right to an individual conviction.

STOCKMANN: (starting) No right to—!

BURGOMASTER: As an official. In your private capacity, of course, it is another matter. But as a subordinate official of the Baths, you have no right to express any conviction opposed to that of your superiors.

STOCKMANN: This is too much! I, a doctor, a man of science, have no right to—!

BURGOMASTER: The matter in question is not a purely scientific one; it is a complex affair, with both a technical and a financial side.

STOCKMANN: What the devil do I care what it is! I will be free to speak my mind on any subject under the sun!

BURGOMASTER: Just as you please—as long as it doesn't concern the Baths. We forbid you to meddle with them.

STOCKMANN: (*shouting*) You forbid—! You! A set of—

BURGOMASTER: *I* forbid it—*I*, your superior; and when I issue an order, you simply have to obey.

STOCKMANN: (*controlling himself*) Upon my word, Peter, if you weren't my brother—

PETRA: (*tearing open the door*) Father, you shan't submit to this!

MRS. STOCKMANN: (*following Petra*) Petra, Petra!

BURGOMASTER: Ah! So we've been listening!

MRS. STOCKMANN: The partition is so thin, we couldn't help it—

PETRA: I stood and listened on purpose.

BURGOMASTER: Well, on the whole, I'm not sorry.

STOCKMANN: (*coming nearer to him*) You spoke to me of forbidding and obeying—

BURGOMASTER: You forced me to adopt that tone.

STOCKMANN: And am I to give myself the lie, in a public declaration?

BURGOMASTER: We consider it absolutely essential that you issue a statement in the terms indicated.

STOCKMANN: And if I do not?

BURGOMASTER: Then we shall issue a statement ourselves to reassure the public.

STOCKMANN: Well and good; then I shall write against you. I shall stick to my point and prove that *I* am right, and you are wrong. And what will you do then?

BURGOMASTER: Then I shall be unable to prevent your dismissal.

STOCKMANN: What—!

MRS. STOCKMANN: Dismissal—

BURGOMASTER: Your dismissal from the Baths. I shall be compelled to move that you be given notice at once, and that you have no connection whatever with the Baths in future.

STOCKMANN: You would dare do that!

BURGOMASTER: You're the one playing the daring game.

PETRA: Uncle, this is a shameful way to treat a man like father.

MRS. STOCKMANN: Do be quiet, Petra.

BURGOMASTER: (*looking at Petra*) So, we have opinions of our own already, eh? To be sure, to be sure. (*To Mrs. Stockmann.*) Sister-in-law, you are presumably the most rational member of this household. Use all your influence with your husband; try to make him realize what this will involve for his family—

STOCKMANN: My family concerns myself alone.

BURGOMASTER: For his family, I say, and for the town he lives in.

STOCKMANN: I am the one with the real good of the town at heart. I want to show up the evils that, sooner or later, must come to light. You shall see whether I love my native town.

BURGOMASTER: You! Why, in your blind obstinacy, you want to cut off the town's chief source of prosperity!

STOCKMANN: That source is poisoned, man! Are you mad? We live by dealing in filth and contamination. The whole of our flourishing life is rooted in a lie.

BURGOMASTER: Imagination—or worse. The man who broadcasts such insinuations against his native town must be an enemy of society.

STOCKMANN: (*going towards him*) You dare to—!

MRS. STOCKMANN: (*coming between them*) Thomas!

PETRA: (*seizing her father's arm*) Father! Keep calm!

BURGOMASTER: I will not expose myself to violence. You have had your warning. Think over what you owe to yourself and to your family. Good-bye. (*He goes out.*)

STOCKMANN: (*walking up and down*) And I must put up with such treatment! And in my own house, Katrina! What do you say to that?

MRS. STOCKMANN: I agree it's a shame and a disgrace, Thomas—

PETRA: Oh, if I could only get hold of uncle—!

STOCKMANN: It's my own fault. I ought to have stood up to them long ago—to have shown my teeth—and used them too! To be called an enemy of society! Me! I won't put up with it; by Heaven I won't!

MRS. STOCKMANN: But my dear Thomas, after all, your brother has the power—

STOCKMANN: Yes, but I am in the right.

MRS. STOCKMANN: Ah, yes, right, right! What good does it do to be in the right, if you haven't any might?

PETRA: Oh, mother—how can you talk like that?

STOCKMANN: What! No good to have right on your side in a free community? What an absurd idea, Katrina. And besides— haven't I got the free and independent press on my side—and the compact majority behind me. That's might enough, I should think.

MRS. STOCKMANN: Why, good heavens, Thomas, you're surely not thinking of—

STOCKMANN: What am I not thinking of?

MRS. STOCKMAN: Thinking of setting yourself up against your brother.

STOCKMANN: What the devil would you have me do, if not stick to the truth?

PETRA: Yes, that's what I'd like to know.

MRS. STOCKMANN: But it will be of no earthly use. If they won't do anything, they won't.

STOCKMANN: (*laughing*) Just wait a while, Katrina, and you'll see whether I can fight my battles to the end.

MRS. STOCKMANN: Yes, to the end of getting your dismissal; that's what will happen.

STOCKMANN: Well, at any rate I'll have done my duty towards the public, towards society—I who have been called an enemy of society!

MRS. STOCKMANN: But towards your family, Thomas? Towards us? Do you think you'll be doing your duty towards those dependent on you?

PETRA: Oh mother, don't always think of us first.

MRS. STOCKMANN: It's easy for you to talk; you can stand alone if you have to. But remember the boys, Thomas; and think a little of yourself too, and of me—

STOCKMANN: You must be out of your senses, Katrina. If I were to be a pitiful coward and knuckle under to Peter and his confounded crew, do you think I would ever have another happy hour in my life?

MRS. STOCKMANN: I don't know about that; but God protect us from the sort of life we shall all have to lead if you go on defying them. There you will be again with nothing to live on, with no regular income. I should have thought we'd had enough of that in the old days. Remember them, Thomas; think of what it all means.

STOCKMANN: (*struggling with himself and clenching his hands*) And is that what these jacks-in-office can do to a free and honest man! Isn't it revolting, Katrina?

MRS. STOCKMANN: Yes, no doubt they are treating you shamefully. But God knows there's plenty of injustice in the world and one must just submit to it.

Eilef and Morten, Stockmann's sons, enter from the hall, with their schoolbooks.

MRS. STOCKMANN: Here are the boys, Thomas. Look at them. What will become of them! Oh, no! You can't have the heart to—

STOCKMANN: The boys—(*His tone changes to one of firmness and decision.*) Never! I don't care if the whole earth crumbles, but I will never bow my neck beneath the yoke. (*He goes towards his room.*)

MRS. STOCKMANN: (*following him*) Thomas—what are you going to do?

STOCKMANN: I must be able to look my boys in the face when they have grown into free men. (*He goes into his room.*)

MRS. STOCKMANN: (*bursting into tears*) Oh, God help us all!

PETRA: Father is completely honourable. He will never give in! *The boys ask wonderingly what it all means; Petra signs to them to be quiet as the curtain falls.*

BACK TO METHUSELAH

(*Act II*)

by

Bernard Shaw

CHARACTERS

ADAM.
EVE.
CAIN.

THE AUTHOR

Bernard Shaw was born in Ireland in 1856 and died in England in 1950. During this time he became a critic, a novelist, a political propagandist (for the socialist cause) and, above all, a dramatist. Today it is as a dramatist that he is most widely known, although it was the latest activity in which he engaged. Like Ibsen, Shaw was interested in social problems, but tackled them from a different point of view, using comedy to demonstrate the absurdity of many conventional attitudes. His later plays tend to deal not so much with specific social problems as with the broad problem of the future of mankind. Such a play is *Back to Methuselah*.

34

THE PLAY

Back to Methuselah was published in the year 1921. It is an enormous play written in five parts, and when it is performed takes three nights at the theatre. It is as Shaw said, 'not a commercial job'. It belongs perhaps more to the theatre of the mind. What inspired him to write it was the effect on thinking of the great naturalist Darwin's theory of natural selection, or the survival of the fittest. The play is thus about evolution. Shaw writes: 'Our will to live depends on hope; for we die of despair, or as I have called it in the Methuselah cycle, discouragement. What damns Darwinian Natural Selection as a creed is that it takes hope out of evolution and substitutes a paralysing fatalism which is utterly discouraging.' The broad theme of the play is that man can will to be better himself, to make the world better. The scene included here is the second act of Part I, set in the Garden of Eden. (The last part of the play is set in the year 31,920 A.D.) The first act of Part I is concerned with Adam and Eve and the Serpent as they discover they have knowledge and can act and will events to happen. Adam is to live a thousand years. In Act II, which follows, several hundred years have passed, and the world has been peopled with the children of Adam and Eve. Their oldest living son Cain comes to call on them.

In this scene Shaw shows the three races of people: the diggers and the peaceful like Adam; the killers (hunters and warriors) like Cain; and the thinkers (artists, poets, musicians, philosophers) like Enoch. In this short parable the future of mankind in Twentieth Century terms is sketched out in the argument between Adam, Eve and Cain.

BACK TO METHUSELAH
Act II

Morning. An oasis in Mesopotamia. Close at hand the end of a log house abuts on a kitchen garden. Adam is digging in the middle of the garden. On his right, Eve sits on a stool in the shadow of a tree by the doorway, spinning flax. Her wheel, which she turns by hand, is a large disc of heavy wood, practically a fly-wheel. At the opposite side of the garden is a thorn brake with a passage through it barred by a hurdle.

The two are scantily and carelessly dressed in rough linen and leaves. They have lost their youth and attractive grace: and Adam has an unkempt beard and jaggedly cut hair; but they are strong and in the prime of life. Adam looks worried, like a farmer. Eve better humoured (having given up worrying), sits and spins and thinks.

A MAN'S VOICE: Hallo, mother!

EVE: (*looking across the garden towards the hurdle*) Here is Cain.

ADAM: (*uttering a grunt of disgust*) !!! (*He goes on digging without raising his head.*)

Cain kicks the hurdle out of his way, and strides into the garden. In pose, voice and dress he is insistently warlike. He is equipped with huge spear and broad brass-bound leather shield. To his parents he has the self-assertive, not-quite-at-ease manner of a revolted son who knows that he is not forgiven or approved of.

CAIN: (*to Adam*) Still digging? Always dig, dig, dig. Sticking in the old furrow. No progress! no advanced ideas! no adventures! What should I be if I had stuck to the digging you taught me?

ADAM: What are you now, with your shield and spear, and your brother's blood crying from the ground against you?

CAIN: I am the first murderer: you are only the first man. Anybody could be the first man: it is as easy as to be the first cabbage. To be the first murderer one must be a man of spirit.

ADAM: Begone. Leave us in peace. The world is wide enough to keep us apart.

EVE: Why do you want to drive him away? He is mine. I made him out of my own body. I want to see my work sometimes.

36

ADAM: You made Abel also. He killed Abel. Can you bear to look at him after that?

CAIN: Whose fault was it that I killed Abel? Who invented killing? Did I? No: he invented it himself. I followed your teaching. I dug and dug and dug. I cleared away the thistles and briars. I ate the fruits of the earth. I lived in the sweat of my brow, as you do. I was a fool. But Abel was a discoverer, a man of ideas, of spirit: a true Progressive. He was the discoverer of blood. He was the inventor of killing. He found out that the fire of the sun could be brought down to a dewdrop. He invented the altar to keep the fire alive. He changed the beasts he killed into meat by the fire of the altar. He kept himself alive by eating meat. His meal cost him a day's glorious health-giving sport and an hour's amusing play with the fire. You learnt nothing from him: you drudged and drudged and drudged, and dug and dug and dug, and made me do the same. I envied his happiness, his freedom. I despised myself for not doing as he did instead of what you did. He became so happy that he shared his meal with the Voice that had whispered all his inventions to him. He said that the Voice was the voice of the fire that cooked his food, and that the fire that could cook could also eat. It was true: I saw the fire consume the food on his altar. Then I, too, made an altar, and offered my food on it, my grains, my roots, my fruit. Useless: nothing happened. He laughed at me; and then came my great idea: why not kill him as he killed the beasts? I struck; and he died, just as they did. Then I gave up your old silly drudging ways, and lived as he had lived, by the chase, by the killing and by the fire. Am I not better than you? stronger, happier, freer?

ADAM: You are not stronger: you are shorter in the wind: you cannot endure. You have made the beasts afraid of us; and the snake has invented poison to protect herself against you. I fear you myself. If you take a step towards your mother with that spear of yours I will strike you with my spade as you struck Abel.

EVE: He will not strike me. He loves me.

ADAM: He loved his brother. But he killed him.

CAIN: I do not want to kill women. I do not want to kill my mother. And for her sake I will not kill you, though I could send this spear through you without coming within reach of your spade. But for her, I could not resist the sport of trying to kill you, in spite of my fear that you would kill me. I have striven with a boar and with a lion as to which of us should kill the other. I have striven with a man: spear to spear and shield to shield. It is terrible; but there is no joy like it. I call it fighting. He who has never fought has never lived. That is what has brought me to my mother today.

ADAM: What have you to do with one another now? She is the creator, you the destroyer.

CAIN: How can I destroy unless she creates? I want her to create more and more men: aye, and more and more women, that they may in turn create more men. I have imagined a glorious poem of many men, of more men than there are leaves on a thousand trees. I will divide them into two great hosts. One of them I will lead; and the other will be led by the man I fear most and desire to fight and kill most. And each host shall try to kill the other host. Think of that! all those multitudes of men fighting, fighting, killing, killing! The four rivers running with blood! The shouts of triumph! the howls of rage! the curses of despair! the shrieks of torment! That will be life indeed: life lived to the very marrow: burning, overwhelming life. Every man who has not seen it, heard it, felt it, risked it, will feel a humbled fool in the presence of the man who has.

EVE: And I! I am to be a mere convenience to make men for you to kill!

CAIN: Mother: the making of men is your right, your risk, your agony, your glory, your triumph. You make my father here your mere convenience, as you call it, for that. He has to dig for you, sweat for you, plod for you, like the ox who helps him to tear up the ground or the ass who carries his burdens for him. No woman shall make me live my father's life. I will hunt: I will fight and strive to the very bursting of my sinews. When we have slain the boar at the risk of my life, I will throw it to my woman to cook, and give her a morsel of it for her pains. She shall have no other food; and that will make her my slave. And the man that slays me shall have her for his booty. Man shall be the master of Woman, not her baby and her drudge.

Adam throws down his spade, and stands looking darkly at Eve.

EVE: Are you tempted, Adam? Does this seem a better thing to you than love between us?

CAIN: What does he know of love? Only when he has fought, when he has faced terror and death, when he has striven to the spending of the last rally of his strength, can he know what it is to rest in love in the arms of a woman. Ask that woman whom you made, who is also my wife, whether she would have me as I was in the days when I followed the ways of Adam, and was a digger and a drudge?

EVE: (*angrily throwing down her distaff*) What! You dare come here boasting about that good-for-nothing Lua, the worst of daughters and the worst of wives! You her master! You are more her slave than Adam's ox or your own sheep dog. Forsooth, when you have slain the boar at the risk of your life, you will throw her a morsel of it for her pains! Ha! Poor wretch: do you think I do not know her, and know you better than that? Do you risk your life when you trap the ermine and the sable and the blue fox to hang on her lazy shoulders and make her look more like an animal than a woman? When you have to snare the little tender birds because it is too much trouble for her to chew honest food, how much of a great warrior do you feel then? You slay the tiger at the risk of your life; but who gets the striped skin you have run that risk for? She takes it to lie on, and flings you the carrion flesh you cannot eat. You fight because you think that your fighting makes her admire and desire you. Fool: she makes you fight because you bring her the ornaments and the treasures of those you have slain, and because she is courted and propitiated with power and gold by the people who fear you. You say that I make a mere convenience of Adam: I who spin and keep the house, and bear and rear children, and am a woman and not a pet animal to please men and prey on them! What are you, you poor slave of a painted face and a bundle of skunk's fur? You were a man-child when I bore you. Lua was a woman-child when I bore her. What have you made of yourselves?

CAIN: (*letting his spear fall into the crook of his shield arm*) There is something higher than man. There is hero and superman.

EVE: Superman! You are no superman: you are Anti-Man: you are to other men what the stoat is to the rabbit; and she is to you what the leech is to the stoat. You despise your father; but when he dies the world will be the richer because he lived. When you die, men will say, 'He was a great warrior; but it would have been better for the world if he had never been born.' And of Lua they will say nothing; but when they think of her they will spit.

CAIN: She is a better sort of woman to live with than you. If Lua nagged at me as you are nagging, and as you nag at Adam,

I would beat her black and blue from head to foot. I have done it too, slave as you say I am.

EVE: Yes, because she looked at another man. And then you grovelled at her feet, and cried, and begged her to forgive you, and were ten times more her slave than ever; and she, when she had finished screaming and the pain went off a little, she forgave you, did she not?

CAIN: She loved me more than ever. That is the true nature of woman.

EVE: (*now pitying him maternally*) Love! You call that love! You call that the true nature of woman! My boy: this is neither man nor woman nor love nor life. You have no real strength in your bones nor sap in your flesh.

CAIN: Ha! (*he seizes his spear and swings it muscularly*).

EVE: Yes: you have to twirl a stick to feel your strength: you cannot taste life without making it bitter and boiling hot: you cannot love Lua until her face is painted, nor feel the natural warmth of her flesh until you have stuck a squirrel's fur on it. You can feel nothing but a torment, and believe nothing but a lie. You will not raise your head to look at all the miracles of life that surround you; but you will run ten miles to see a fight or a death.

ADAM: Enough said. Let the boy alone.

CAIN: Boy! Ha! ha!

EVE: (*to Adam*) You think, perhaps, that his way of life may be better than yours after all. You are still tempted. Well, will you pamper me as he pampers his woman? Will you kill tigers and bears until I have a heap of their skins to lounge on? Shall I paint my face and let my arms waste into pretty softness, and eat partridges and doves, and the flesh of kids whose milk you will steal for me?

ADAM: You are hard enough to bear with as you are. Stay as you are; and I will stay as I am.

CAIN: You neither of you know anything about life. You are simple country folk. You are the nurses and valets of the oxen and dogs and asses you have tamed to work for you. I can raise you out of that. I have a plan. Why not tame men and women to work for us? Why not bring them up from childhood never to know any other lot, so that they may believe that we are gods, and that they are here only to make life glorious for us?

ADAM: (*impressed*) That is a great thought, certainly.

EVE: (*contemptuously*) Great thought!

ADAM: Well, as the serpent used to say, why not?

EVE: Because I would not have such wretches in my house. Because I hate creatures with two heads, or with withered limbs, or that are distorted and perverted and unnatural. I have told Cain already that he is not a man and that Lua is not a woman: they are monsters. And now you want to make still more unnatural monsters, so that you may be utterly lazy and worthless, and that your tamed human animals may find work a blasting curse. A fine dream, truly! (*To Cain*) Your father is a fool skin deep; but you are a fool to your very marrow; and your baggage of a wife is worse.

ADAM: Why am I a fool? How am I a greater fool than you?

EVE: You said there would be no killings because the Voice would tell our children that they must not kill. Why did it not tell Cain that?

CAIN: It did; but I am not a child to be afraid of a Voice. The Voice thought I was nothing but my brother's keeper. It found that I was myself, and that it was for Abel to be himself also, and look to himself. He was not my keeper any more than I was his: why did he not kill me? There was no more to prevent him than there was to prevent me: it was man to man; and I won. I was the first conqueror.

ADAM: What did the Voice say to you when you thought all that?

CAIN: Why, it gave me right. It said that my deed was as a mark on me, a burnt-in ma·k such as Abel put on his sheep, that no man should slay me. And here I stand unslain, whilst the cowards who have never slain, the men who are content to be their brothers' keepers instead of their masters, are despised and rejected, and slain like rabbits. He who bears the brand of Cain shall rule the earth. When he falls, he shall be avenged sevenfold: the Voice has said it; so beware how you plot against me, you and all the rest.

ADAM: Cease your boasting and bullying, and tell the truth. Does not the Voice tell you that as no man dare slay you foɪ murdering your brother, you ought to slay yourself?

CAIN: No.

ADAM: Then there is no such thing as divine justice, unless you are lying.

CAIN: I am not lying: I dare all truths. There is divine justice. For the Voice tells me that I must offer myself to every man to be killed if he can kill me. Without danger I cannot be great. That is how I pay for Abel's blood. Danger and fear follow my steps everywhere. Without them courage would have no sense. And it is courage, courage, courage, that raises the blood of life to crimson splendour.

ADAM: (*picking up his spade and preparing to dig again*) Take yourself off then. This splendid life of yours does not last for a thousand years; and I must last for a thousand years. When you fighters do not get killed in fighting one another or fighting the beasts, you die from mere evil in yourselves. Your flesh ceases to grow like man's flesh; it grows like a fungus on a tree. Instead of breathing, you sneeze, or cough up your insides, and wither and perish. Your bowels become rotten; your hair falls from you; your teeth blacken and drop out; and you die before your time, not because you will, but because you must. I will dig and live.

CAIN: And pray, what use is this thousand years of life to you, you old vegetable? Do you dig any better because you have been digging for hundreds of years? I have not lived as long as you; but I know all there is to be known of the craft of digging. By quitting it I have set myself free to learn nobler crafts of which you know nothing. I know the craft of fighting and of hunting: in a word, the craft of killing. What certainty have you of your thousand years? I could kill both of you; and you could no more defend yourselves than a couple of sheep. I spare you; but others may kill you. Why not live bravely, and die early and make room for others? Why, I—I! that know many more crafts than either of you, am tired of myself when I am not fighting or hunting. Sooner than face a thousand years of it I should kill myself as the Voice sometimes tempts me to do already.

ADAM: Liar: you denied just now that it called on you to pay for Abel's life with your own.

CAIN: The Voice does not speak to me as it does to you. I am a man: you are only a grown-up child. One does not speak to a child as to a man. And man does not listen and tremble in silence. He replies: he makes the Voice respect him: in the end he dictates what the Voice shall say.

ADAM: May your tongue be accurst for such blasphemy!

EVE: Keep a guard on your own tongue; and do not curse my son. It was Lilith who did wrong when she shared the labor of creation so unequally between man and wife. If you, Cain, had had the trouble of making Abel, or had had to make another man to replace him when he was gone, you would not have killed him: you would have risked your own life to save his. That is why all this empty talk of yours, which tempted Adam just now when he threw down his spade and listened to you for a while, went by me like foul wind that has passed over a dead body. That is why there is enmity between Woman the creator and Man the destroyer. I know you: I am your mother. You are idle: you are selfish. It is long and hard and painful to create life: it is short and easy to steal the life others have made. When you dug, you made the earth live and bring forth as I live and bring forth. It was for that that Lilith set you free from the Travail of women, not for theft and murder.

CAIN: The Devil thank her for it! I can make better use of my time than to play the husband to the clay beneath my feet.

ADAM: Devil? What new word is that?

CAIN: Hearken to me, old fool. I have never in my soul listened willingly when you have told me of the Voice that whispers to you. There must be two Voices: one that gulls and despises you, and another that trusts and respects me. I call yours the Devil. Mine I call the Voice of God.

ADAM: Mine is the Voice of Life: yours the Voice of Death.

CAIN: Be it so. For it whispers to me that death is not really death: that it is the gate of another life: a life infinitely splendid and intense: a life of the soul alone: a life without clods or spades, hunger or fatigue—

EVE: Selfish and idle, Cain. I know.

CAIN: Selfish, yes: a life in which no man is his brother's keeper, because his brother can keep himself. But am I idle? In rejecting your drudgery, have I not embraced evils and agonies of which you know nothing? The arrow is lighter in the hand than the spade; but the energy that drives it through the breast of the fighter is as fire to water compared with the strength that drives the spade into the harmless dirty clay. My strength is as the strength of ten because my heart is pure.

ADAM: What is that word? What is pure?

CAIN: Turned from the clay. Turned upward to the sun, to the clear clean heavens.

ADAM: The heavens are empty, child. The earth is fruitful. The earth feeds us. It gives us the strength by which we made you and all mankind. Cut off from the clay which you despise, you would perish miserably.

CAIN: I revolt against the clay. I revolt against the food. You say it gives us strength: does it not also turn into filth and smite us with diseases? I revolt against these births that you and mother are so proud of. They drag us down to the level of the beasts. If that is to be the last thing as it has been the first, let mankind perish. If I am to eat like a bear, if Lua is to bring forth cubs like a bear, then I had rather be a bear than a man; for the bear is not ashamed: he knows no better. If you are content, like the bear, I am not. Stay with the woman who gives you children: I will go to the woman who gives me dreams. Grope in the ground for your food: I will bring it from the skies with my arrows, or strike it down as it roams the earth in the pride of its life. If I must have food or die, I will at least have it at as far a remove from the earth as I can. The ox shall make it something nobler than grass before it comes to me. And as the man is nobler than the ox, I shall some day let my enemy eat the ox; and then I will slay and eat him.

ADAM: Monster! You hear this Eve?

EVE: So that is what comes of turning your face to the clean clear heavens! Man-eating! Child-eating! For that is what it would come to, just as it came to lambs and kids when Abel began with sheep and goats. You are a poor silly creature after all. Do you think I never have these thoughts: I! who have the labor of child-bearing: I! who have the drudgery of preparing food? I thought for a moment that perhaps this strong brave son of mine, who could imagine something better, and could desire what he imagined, might also be able to will what he desired until he created it. And all that comes of it is that he wants to be a bear and eat children. Even a bear would not eat a man if it could get honey instead.

CAIN: I do not want to be a bear. I do not want to eat children. I do not know what I want, except that I want to be something higher and nobler than this stupid old digger whom Lilith made to help you to bring me into the world, and whom you despise now that he has served your turn.

ADAM: (*in sullen rage*) I have half a mind to shew you that my spade can split your undutiful head open, in spite of your spear.

CAIN: Undutiful! Ha! ha! (*Flourishing his spear*) Try it, old everybody's father. Try a taste of fighting.

EVE: Peace, peace, you two fools. Sit down and be quiet; and listen to me. (*Adam, with a weary shrug, throws down his spade. Cain, with a laughing one, throws down his shield and spear. Both sit on the ground*.) I hardly know which of you satisfies me least, you with your dirty digging, or he with his dirty killing. I cannot think it was for either of these cheap ways of life that Lilith set you free. (*To Adam*) You dig roots and coax grains out of the earth: why do you not draw down a divine sustenance from the skies? He steals and kills for his food; and makes up idle poems of life after death; and dresses up his terror-ridden life with fine words and disease-ridden body with fine clothes, so that men may glorify and honour him instead of cursing him as murderer and thief. All you men, except only Adam, are my sons, or my sons' sons, or my sons' sons' sons: you all come to see me: you all shew off before me: all your little wisdoms and accomplishments are trotted out before mother Eve. The diggers come: the fighters and killers come: they are both very dull; for they either complain to me of the last harvest, or boast to me of the last fight; and one harvest is just like another, and the last fight only a repetition of the first. Oh, I have heard it all a thousand times. They tell me too of their last-born: the clever thing the darling child said yesterday, and how much more wonderful or witty or quaint it is than any child that ever was born before. And I have to pretend to be surprised, delighted, interested; though the last child is like the first, and has said and done nothing that did not delight Adam and me when you and Abel said it. For you were the first children in the world, and filled us with such wonder and delight as no couple can ever again feel while the world lasts. When I can bear no more, I go to our old garden, that is now a mass of nettles and thistles, in the hope of finding the serpent to talk to. But you have made the serpent our enemy: she has left the garden, or is dead: I never see her now. So I have to come back and listen to Adam saying the same thing for the ten-thousandth time, or to receive a visit from the last great-great-grandson who has grown up and wants to impress me with his importance. Oh, it is dreary, dreary! And there is yet nearly seven hundred years of it to endure.

CAIN: Poor mother! You see, life is too long. One tires of everything. There is nothing new under the sun.

ADAM: (*to Eve, grumpily*) Why do you live on, if you can find nothing better to do than complain?

EVE: Because there is still hope.

CAIN: Of What?

EVE: Of the coming true of your dreams and mine. Of newly

created things. Of better things. My sons and my sons' sons are not all diggers and fighters. Some of them will neither dig nor fight: they are more useless than either of you: they are weaklings and cowards: they are vain; yet they are dirty and will not take the trouble to cut their hair. They borrow and never pay; but one gives them what they want because they tell beautiful lies in beautiful words. They can remember their dreams. They can dream without sleeping. They have not will enough to create instead of dreaming; but the serpent said that every dream could be willed into creation by those strong enough to believe in it. There are others who cut reeds of different lengths and blow through them, making lovely patterns of sound in the air; and some of them can weave the patterns together, sounding three reeds at the same time, and raising my soul to things for which I have no words. And others make little mammoths out of clay, or make faces appear on flat stones, and ask me to create women for them with such faces. I have watched those faces and willed; and then I have made a woman-child that has grown up quite like them. And others think of numbers without having to count on their fingers, and watch the sky at night, and give names to the stars, and can foretell when the sun will be covered with a black saucepan lid. And there is Tubal, who made this wheel for me which has saved me so much labor. And there is Enoch, who walks on the hills, and hears the Voice continually, and has given up his will to do the will of the Voice, and has some of the Voice's greatness. When they come, there is always some new wonder, or some new hope: something to live for. They never want to die, because they are always learning and always creating either things of wisdom, or at least dreaming of them. And then you, Cain, come to me with your stupid fighting and destroying, and your foolish boasting; and you want me to tell you that it is all splendid, and that you are heroic, and that nothing but death or the dread of death makes life worth living. Away with you, naughty child; and do you, Adam, go on with your work and not waste your time listening to him.

CAIN: I am not, perhaps, very clever; but—

EVE: (*interrupting him*) Perhaps not; but do not begin to boast of that. It is no credit to you.

CAIN: For all that, mother, I have an instinct which tells me that death plays a part in life. Tell me this: who invented death?

Adam springs to his feet. Eve drops her distaff. Both show the greatest consternation.

CAIN: What is the matter with you both?

ADAM: Boy: you have asked us a terrible question.

EVE: You invented murder. Let that be enough for you.

CAIN: Murder is not death. You know what I mean. Those whom I slay would die if I spared them. If I am not slain, yet shall I die. Who put this upon me? I say, who invented death?

ADAM: Be reasonable, boy. Could you bear to live for ever? You think you could, because you know that you will never have to make your thought good. But I have known what it is to sit and brood under the terror of eternity, of immortality. Think of it, man: to have no escape! to be Adam, Adam, Adam through more days than there are grains of sand by the two rivers, and then be as far from the end as ever! I, who have so much in me that I hate and long to cast off! Be thankful to your parents, who enabled you to hand on your burden to new and better men, and won for you an eternal rest; for it was we who invented death.

CAIN: (*rising*) You did well: I, too, do not want to live for ever. But, if you invented death, why do you blame me, who am a minister of death?

ADAM: I do not blame you. Go in peace. Leave me to my digging, and your mother to her spinning.

CAIN: Well, I will leave you to it, though I have shewn you a better way. (*He picks up his shield and spear.*) I will go back to my brave warrior friends and their splendid women. (*He strides to the thorn brake.*) When Adam delved and Eve span, who was then the gentle man? (*He goes away roaring with laughter, which ceases as he cries from the distance*) Good-bye, mother.

ADAM: (*grumbling*) He might have put the hurdle back, lazy hound! (*He replaces the hurdle across the passage.*)

EVE: Through him and his like, death is gaining on life. Already most of our grandchildren die before they have sense enough to know how to live.

ADAM: No matter (*He spits on his hands, and takes up the spade again.*) Life is still long enough to learn to dig, short as they are making it.

EVE: (*musing*) Yes, to dig. And to fight. But is it long enough for the other things, the great things? Will they live long enough to eat manna?

ADAM: What is manna?

EVE: Food drawn down from heaven, made out of air, not dug dirtily from the earth. Will they learn all the ways of all the stars in their little time? It took Enoch two hundred years to learn to interpret the will of the Voice. When he was a mere child of eighty, his babyish attempts to understand the Voice were more dangerous than the wrath of Cain. If they shorten their lives, they will dig and fight and kill and die; and their baby Enochs will tell them that it is the will of the Voice that they should dig and fight and kill and die for ever.

ADAM: If they are lazy and have a will towards death I cannot help it. I will live my thousand years: if they will not, let them die and be damned.

EVE: Damned? What is that?

ADAM: The state of them that love death more than life. Go on with your spinning; and do not sit there idle while I am straining my muscles for you.

EVE: (*slowly taking up her distaff*) If you were not a fool you would find something better for both of us to live by than this spinning and digging.

ADAM: Go on with your work, I tell you; or you shall go without bread.

EVE: Man need not always live by bread alone. There is something else. We do not yet know what it is; but some day we shall find out; and then we will live on that alone; and there shall be no more digging nor spinning, nor fighting nor killing.

She spins resignedly. He digs impatiently.

Twentieth Century Comedy

TOBIAS AND THE ANGEL

(Act I, Scene II)

by

James Bridie

CHARACTERS

TOBIAS, *A poor Jewish boy*
THE ARCHANGEL RAPHAEL, *Thought by Tobias to be a servant, Azarias.*
A KURDISH BANDIT.
TOBY, *Tobias' Dog.*

THE AUTHOR

James Bridie is the pen-name of Dr. O. H. Mavor, who is Scotland's best known playwright of the twentieth century. He was born in Glasgow in 1888, and although working almost constantly as a medical practitioner, produced a stream of plays remarkable for their wit and strong moral purpose. Some of the best-known are *The Anatomist, Tobias and the Angel, A Sleeping Clergyman, Storm in a Teacup, Susannah and the Elders* and *Mr. Bolfry.* The last-mentioned is a hilarious play about the visit of the devil to a Presbyterian minister's house in the Scottish Highlands. Bridie's wit is completely his own and consists of treating extraordinary events in a matter-of-fact way. He also has a genius for creating memorable characters who all talk 'twenty to the dozen', delighting audiences with their fluent repartee. Unfortunately, it appears that Bridie wrote too many plays, for numbers of them are carelessly constructed and fade away after promising beginnings.

THE PLAY

Tobias and the Angel is one of Bridie's most amusing plays. It is based on a story from the *Book of Tobit*, a popular story of romance and legend from the *Apocrypha*, a collection of Jewish or Christian writings not considered divinely inspired and not included, therefore, in the Bible. Tobias, the son of a poor Jew who has once been wealthy, is a plump young man mainly notable for his lack of courage. His family is visited by the Archangel Raphael who disguises himself as a servant and accompanies Tobias on a dangerous journey to Persia. With the Archangel's help, he arrives safely, and proceeds to fall in love with Sara, the daughter of an old friend of his father. Unfortunately, one of the fallen angels, Asmoday, is also in love with her and has killed her seven previous husbands. Once again, Raphael makes it possible for Tobias to survive, and he and Sara are married.

The scene included here (Act I Scene II), illustrates Bridie's method of creating comedy. The situation is an extraordinary one, but it is dealt with in a perfectly straightforward manner. It also shows Bridie's skill in writing literate and amusing dialogue—note particularly Tobias' harangue to the bandit.

TOBIAS AND THE ANGEL

Act I, Scene II

The scene is the east bank of the Tigris, almost a day's march from Nineveh. Above the ridge of the bank, the sky tapers up from dusty brass, through bronze and olive-green to bright blue. No horizon is seen.

Tobias, tired and hot, is sitting on his pack. Raphael is standing with his back to the auditorium looking across the Tigris. He, too, has taken off his pack.

RAPHAEL: Are you tired?

TOBIAS: Tired! My back and legs are made of aches and pains instead of bones and muscles. My feet are red-hot. My stomach is flopping about my ankles. The only light thing about me is my head.

RAPHAEL: You must be in very inferior training.

TOBIAS: Well, you see, I spend most of this part of the year sleeping in the shade of the Governor's date palms. I am not very much used to walking.

RAPHAEL: I am not used to walking either.

TOBIAS: I should have thought you were. How do you get about? You fly, I suppose?

RAPHAEL: Yes.

TOBIAS: I see. You are going to tell me another story. I like your stories very much, Azarias, but don't you think we could have something to eat?

RAPHAEL: Not yet. You are too hot and tired. It would make you ill. I think a swim would freshen you up. Can you swim?

TOBIAS: It is very nearly the only thing I can do. I would have made a very good trout.

RAPHAEL: Well, take your clothes off and get into the river.

TOBIAS: Now that is what I should call a good idea. Isn't it Tobykins? Are you hot and dusty too, old dog? Come and have a nice swim with master. I say, you are full of good ideas, Azarias. Are you coming in too?

RAPHAEL: No. Not just now.

TOBIAS: Oh, why not?

RAPHAEL: If you must know, I have a slight abnormality in the region of my shoulder-blades. Nothing much, but I am sensitive on these matters. I always bathe alone.

TOBIAS: You are a funny chap. I have two birth-marks and a crop of pimples, but it doesn't worry me. I don't see why any thingummy on your shoulder-blades should worry you.

RAPHAEL: Will you kindly change the subject?

TOBIAS: What is it? Psoriasis?

RAPHAEL: Get into the water. We have a fair distance to go before nightfall.

TOBIAS: Righto. You *are* a bully, Azarias.

Tobias disappears below the ridge, the dog with him.

TOBIAS: (*his head and shoulders appearing over the ridge*) I'll tell you what you are like, Azarias. You are like a cock-eyed cannibal my father had for a valet when we were camel-borne gentry. Rasik, his name was. The cheek he used to give the old man. I would have had him bastinadoed. But I think it would have hurt the old man just as much as it hurt Rasik. I honestly do. Isn't he quaint, the old man? Arranging about your salary and so on as if he were still a millionaire living in Leviathan Avenue instead of . . . Come along, Tobykins. I'm ready if you are. Let's dive together.

A splash. Barks and shrieks of delight.

TOBIAS' VOICE: Do come in, Azarias. It's gorgeous. Ouch! It's like heaven with the lid off.

RAPHAEL: Don't swim out too far. There are nasty currents in the fairway. (*He begins to make a fire.*)

TOBIAS' VOICE: What say?

RAPHAEL: I said, don't swim out too far.

TOBIAS' VOICE: Oh, I'm all right. I'm very much all right. No . . . I'm not. What's this? Azarias, help! The fish, the fish! Oh, Azarias, it's swimming round me. It's looking for a place to bite. It's snapping at me. Oh, Azarias, its teeth! Its teeth!

RAPHAEL: Don't be a coward. Catch it by the little bags behind its jaw—and hold on!

TOBIAS' VOICE: I can't. I can't. Keep away, you brute.

RAPHAEL: Do as I tell you. . .

TOBIAS' VOICE: It's all very well . . . Ough! I've got him. By gum, he is strong!

RAPHAEL: Hold on. Hold on tight.

The dog, dripping with water, is projected over the ridge.

RAPHAEL: That's right. Give him a heave and pitch him on to the bank. Now grip him again.

TOBIAS' VOICE: I've got him. I've hit him with my stick. He's dead. By gum, what a monster.

He appears, naked except for a loincloth, dragging a gigantic mud-fish.

TOBIAS: That's him.

RAPHAEL: That's he, you mean.

TOBIAS: He, then. By gum, he gave me a tough fight. It was a bad day for him when he tried to bite me. I hung on like grim death. I'm slow to take hold, but I never let go. That's t' sort of man I am. Look at him. There's been nothing like him since the whale coughed up Jonas. Ho! If Jonas had been half the man I am he would have swallowed the whale. Isn't he beautiful, Azarias?

RAPHAEL: He is as beautiful as you are marvellous. The fire is ready for him. You will gut the fish and cook him and cut him into steaks and dry them in the sun. They will be useful on the journey.

TOBIAS: *I* will cook him? Look here, Azarias, am I the hired man or are you?

RAPHAEL: I am the hired man. I am paid to guide you, and therefore you will do as I direct. Take your knife and gut the fish.

TOBIAS: Oh, very well.

He follows Raphael's instructions.

RAPHAEL: Here is a cloth. Take first his liver and his gall and wrap them up.

TOBIAS: Why?

RAPHAEL: Because I say so. Put them in your pack.

TOBIAS: But why, Azarias? Please tell me why.

RAPHAEL: One never knows when they may come in handy.

TOBIAS: What is the use of a mud-fish's liver?

RAPHAEL: That is at once a physiological and a philosophical problem, Tobias, and I prefer not to answer it at present. Instead I shall tell you a story while you work. . .

TOBIAS: Thank you very much indeed.

RAPHAEL: Not at all . . . Once upon a time there was a king's daughter who had eyes like two full moons, teeth like a flock of Angora goats, and cheeks like a parcel of pomegranates swimming in blood.

TOBIAS: By gum, she must have been a pretty girl.

RAPHAEL: She was a lovely lady. But one day she fell ill and faded like a sick papyrus lily in the drought. She became pale and wan and could not move from her couch for the fluttering of her heart. The king's magicians . . .

TOBIAS: A friend of mine once knew a girl who was taken badly that way. She could hardly . . .

RAPHAEL: The king's magicians did what they could. They cast her horoscope not once but many times. They sacrificed a bat, a scorpion, a bull and an adder. They bled two hundred slaves till they died. They gave her a decoction of herbs picked during the transit of Mercury and administered three times a day, with suitable incantations, before food.

TOBIAS: And it was of no use?

RAPHAEL: I should not go the length of saying that, Tobias, but it didn't help the king's daughter. She grew daily worse and worse. The king was at his wits' end.

TOBIAS: How sad for the poor old gentleman.

RAPHAEL: On the borders of his kingdom there dwelt a wood-cutter in a mean hut. His youngest son was called Sarabias. He was a half-wit. The two brothers of Sarabias, who were called Arphaxad and Shimsham . . .

TOBIAS: I beg your pardon, I did not catch the second brother's name.

RAPHAEL: Shimsham. Arphaxad and Shimsham, the brothers of Sarabias, one day made a feast. They ate for the feast a braxy ram.

TOBIAS: Why a braxy ram?

RAPHAEL: They were glad to get it. As was their custom, they threw the offal to Sarabias, who sat by the door in the sun. At that moment one of the king's trumpeters passed rehearsing the latest news from the palace.

TOBIAS: And what was the latest news?

RAPHAEL: That the king's daughter had had nothing to eat for seven days and seven nights. Sarabias was sorry to hear this, and, taking up the liver of the braxy ram, he made what speed he could to the palace.

A Kurdish bandit appears behind Raphael's back. His appearance strikes Tobias with terror, as well it may. He is armed to the teeth.

TOBIAS: Oh, *look*, Azarias! Look! Look!
Raphael stops his story and looks at his hands. He does not turn round.

BANDIT: *Salaam aleikum.* I perceive you have been indulging in the gentle pastime of angling. A happy sport, by Allah! And perhaps the one a judicious person would choose for his last day on earth. For most unfortunately you have chosen the stretch of river held sacred by my fathers to pollute it with your lines and bait. So you must die, you two young men. And die, I fear, most horribly. But I am a humane man, and as I see, sir, that you are a foul Jehudi, I can only conclude that, like the rest of your repulsive race, you are dripping with gold, jewels and precious stones. To pass the time pleasantly for a few minutes, I am prepared to bargain with you for what no doubt you consider your not entirely worthless lives. Otherwise my duty will impel me to hang you head downwards over your little fire and cut you slowly to death with little cuts.

TOBIAS: What shall we do? Oh, what shall we do?

RAPHAEL: (*sotto voce*) What an abominable taste in rhetoric he has. He is Mirza Khan, a Kurdish thief. Tell him to go to Gehannum.

TOBIAS: But he might not like it. He has a face like a devil.

RAPHAEL: Tell him so. Tell him what you have done this afternoon.

BANDIT: How unmannerly to whisper. What lack of breeding. Come now, little one, I had the honour to address myself to you. Will you answer before I grow impatient?

RAPHAEL: Answer him. Be a man.

TOBIAS: Do you know what I have been doing this afternoon?

BANDIT: I do not. But it will have a certain pathetic interest. What have you been doing this afternoon?

TOBIAS: I went down to that little gutter-ditch and walked about upon it. And the first thing I met was a huge and scaly monster which thought, as you think, you ignorant dog, that I was a little no-account. And it barked and roared and bit at me. So I killed it and tore out its liver, and there it is wrapped up in a cloth. (*He indicates his enormous pack.*) And what I did to that atrocious, fire-breathing river demon I shall do to you, you hairy-toed polecat, you son of a burnt father, for I am only beginning the carnage I feel I must make before sunset.

BANDIT: Who are you, my lord?

TOBIAS: I am Suleiman-ibn-Daoud, and this is one of my Afreets. Now depart in peace and trouble me no further.

BANDIT: If my lord pleases, I had no idea . . .

TOBIAS: May your blood turn to dog's blood, you father of sixty dogs! Did you hear me tell you to go in peace? Your liver is too white to put beside that of a river dragon, for it is the colour of the dark flames of hell. You are safe from me, pitiful and hideous ape. Only take your ugliness from my pure sight before I repent my mercy.

BANDIT: Allah, have pity on a poor ill-used man. Allah protect you, my lord. (*He withdraws rapidly.*)

TOBIAS: Oh, Azarias, will it be all like this? Will it be all like this, our journey?

RAPHAEL: How can I tell?

TOBIAS: But we have scarcely started, and I have not only been dog-weary and footsore, but twice in deadly peril of my life.

RAPHAEL: All life is perilous. Go ahead and cook the fish.

TOBIAS: I couldn't possibly eat a bite.

RAPHAEL: Very well then, give it to me and I will put it in my pack. It is cooler now. We must be going.

TOBIAS: But this isn't the least what I pictured a journey.

RAPHAEL: Nothing is the least as we picture it.

TOBIAS: I shall have a nervous breakdown long before we reach Media. I feel quite ill already.

RAPHAEL: Nonsense. You did very well. I am quite proud of my little master.

TOBIAS: Are you really? I certainly seemed to be able to speak up to that bandit once I got started. I told him off properly, I think. The words seemed to come, somehow. I heard them at the jetty, but I hoped I had forgotten them. And I did very well with the fish too, didn't I?

RAPHAEL: Yes. But there was no need to lie to the bandit.

TOBIAS: I didn't lie to him.

RAPHAEL: You did. Your story of the fish I forgive you. Everybody exaggerates about fish. But you said you were Solomon. That is very far from being true.

TOBIAS: I didn't know what I was saying. I was excited. I wish I weren't such a coward. I'm afraid of everything, really. I'm even afraid of women.

RAPHAEL: Are you now?

TOBIAS: Indeed I am.

RAPHAEL: Don't you like them?

TOBIAS: Very much, but they terrify me.

RAPHAEL: I think then there is at least one more terrifying adventure in store for you. Let us go.

TOBIAS: What do you mean?

RAPHAEL: (*laughing*) Nothing, nothing.

TOBIAS: I was right in one thing I said to the bandit.

RAPHAEL: What was that?

TOBIAS: I said you were an old Afreet. So you are.

RAPHAEL: There are no such things as Afreets. Come along.

They trudge out, the dog following.

BLITHE SPIRIT

(An excerpt from Act I, Scene II)

by

Noel Coward

CHARACTERS

CHARLES CONDOMINE, *a middle-aged novelist.*
RUTH CONDOMINE, *his second wife.*
DOCTOR BRADMAN, *a friend of the Condomines.*
MRS. BRADMAN, *his wife.*
MADAME ARCARTI, *a medium.*
ELVIRA, *the ghost of Charles' first wife.*

THE AUTHOR

Noel Coward was born in 1899, and is one of the most famous of living playwrights. He has been an actor, producer, film director, composer and song-writer, as well as a straight playwright, and during the 1920s he had five plays running in London at once. For many people he represents the spirit of the 'roaring twenties' in England, but the best of his plays are genuine comedies of manners in the tradition of Sheridan and Wilde. Some of his best known plays are *The Vortex*, *Hay Fever*, *Present Laughter*, *Private Lives* and *Blithe Spirit*, while one of the best films produced in Britain, *Brief Encounter*, was based on a play of his. Coward still writes for the theatre and acts occasionally in films, but he has not been able to repeat his success of the period 1925-45.

THE PLAY

Blithe Spirit, written in 1941, is perhaps Coward's best play. It tells the story of Charles Condomine, a novelist, whose first wife, Elvira, died seven years before the action of the play begins. He has married again and Ruth, his second wife, has provided him

with a comfortable home and relaxed surroundings. This is all changed when he invites a local eccentric, Madame Arcati, to hold a séance in his home to provide him with background material for a new book. At the end of the séance, Elvira appears, but can only be seen and heard by Charles. He now has both his wives in the house at once, and his first problem is to convince Ruth of Elvira's presence. He succeeds in this and Ruth then attempts to rid the house of this 'blithe spirit'. This proves extremely difficult, and slowly Ruth begins to realize that Elvira is trying to kill Charles so that they may be together in the 'other world' for ever. Eventually, Elvira tampers with the steering of the car, but her plan misfires when Ruth drives off in it and is killed. Madame Arcati now attempts to rid the house of Elvira, but only succeeds in conjuring up Ruth's spirit as well. Charles now has the ghosts of both his wives in the house, but towards the end of the play Madame Arcati manages to get rid of them—or at least their visible and audible aspects. The play ends with a hilarious scene, in which Charles talks to the two women, now invisible and inaudible, who systematically wreck the room.

The scene included here, is the séance scene during which Madame Arcati conjures up the spirit of Elvira. It shows Coward at his best, witty, urbane and intensely theatrical.

BLITHE SPIRIT

An excerpt from Act I, Scene II

The scene is the living room of the Condomine's house in Kent. It is light, attractive and comfortably furnished. On the left there are french windows opening on to the garden. On the right there is an open fireplace. At the back there are double doors leading to the hall, the stairs and the servants' quarters. It is evening, after dinner, and Ruth (Mrs. Condomine), Mrs. Bradman and Madame Arcati are having coffee. Charles (Mr. Condomine) and Dr. Bradman enter from the hall.

CHARLES: Well, Madame Arcati—the time is drawing near.

MADAME ARCATI: Who knows? It may be receding!

CHARLES: How very true.

BRADMAN: I hope you feel in the mood, Madame Arcati.

MADAME ARCATI: It isn't a question of mood. It's a question of concentration.

RUTH: You must forgive us being impatient. We can perfectly easily wait though, if you're not quite ready to start.

MADAME ARCATI: Nonsense, my dear, I'm absolutely ready. (*She rises.*) Heigho, heigho, to work we go!

CHARLES: Is there anything you'd like us to do?

MADAME ARCATI: Do?

CHARLES: Yes, hold hands or anything?

MADAME ARCATI: All that will come later. (*She goes to the window.*) First, a few deep, deep breaths of fresh air—You may talk if you wish, it will not disturb me in the least. (*She flings the windows wide open and inhales deeply and a trifle noisily.*)

RUTH: (*with a quizzical glance at Charles*) Oh dear!

CHARLES: (*putting his finger to his lips warningly*) An excellent dinner darling. I congratulate you.

RUTH: The mousse wasn't quite right.

CHARLES: It looked a bit hysterical, but it tasted delicious.

MADAME ARCATI: That cuckoo is very angry. Listen.

They all listen obediently.

CHARLES: How can you tell?

MADAME ARCATI: Timbre. No moon; that's as well, I think. There's mist rising from the marshes. (*A thought strikes her.*) There's no need for me to light my bicycle lamp, is there? I mean, nobody is likely to fall over it?

RUTH: No, we're not expecting anybody else.

MADAME ARCATI: Good night, you foolish bird. (*She closes the windows.*) You have a table?

CHARLES: Yes, we thought that one would do. (*To Ruth*) You told Edith we didn't want to be disturbed?

RUTH: Yes, darling.

MADAME ARCATI: (*walking about the room, twisting and untwisting her hands*) This is a moment I always hate.

RUTH: Are you nervous?

MADAME ARCATI: Yes. When I was a girl I always used to be sick.

BRADMAN: How fortunate you grew out of it.

RUTH: (*hurriedly*) Children are always more prone to be sick than grown-ups, though, aren't they? I know I could never travel in a train with any degree of safety until I was fourteen.

MADAME ARCATI: (*still walking*) 'Little Tommy Tucker sings for his supper. What shall he have but brown bread and butter?' I despise that because it doesn't rhyme at all; but Daphne loves it.

BRADMAN: Who's Daphne?

RUTH: Daphne is Madame Arcati's control. She's a little girl.

BRADMAN: Oh, I see—yes, of course.

CHARLES: How old is she?

MADAME ARCATI: Rising seven when she died.

MRS. BRADMAN: And when was that?

MADAME ARCATI: February the sixth, eighteen eighty-four.

MRS. BRADMAN: Poor little thing.

BRADMAN: She must be a bit long in the tooth by now, I should think.

MADAME ARCATI: (*stopping walking and addressing Dr. Bradman*) You should think, Dr. Bradman, but I fear you don't; at least not profoundly enough.

MRS. BRADMAN: Do be quiet, George. You'll put Madame Arcati off.

MADAME ARCATI: Don't worry, my dear, I am quite used to sceptics. They generally turn out to be the most vulnerable and receptive in the long run.

RUTH: You'd better take that warning to heart, Dr. Bradman.

BRADMAN: Please forgive me, Madame Arcati. I assure you I am most deeply interested.

MADAME ARCATI: It is of no consequence. Will you all sit round the table, please, and place your hands downwards on it?

RUTH: Come, Mrs. Bradman—

CHARLES: What about the lights?

MADAME ARCATI: All in good time, Mr. Condomine. Sit down, please.

The four of them sit down at each side of the séance table. Madame Arcati surveys them critically, her head on one side. She is whistling a little tune. Then she sings.

MADAME ARCATI: The fingers should be touching—that's right. I presume that that is the gramophone, Mr. Condomine?

CHARLES: (*half rising*) Yes. Would you like me to start it? It's an electric one.

MADAME ARCATI: Please stay where you are. I can manage. (*She moves to the gramophone and picks up the record album from the rack below it.*) Now let me see—what have we here? Brahms —oh dear me, no; Rachmaninoff—too florid. Where is the dance music?

RUTH: They're the loose ones on the left.

MADAME ARCATI: I see. (*She stoops down and produces a pile of dance records.*)

CHARLES: I'm afraid they're none of them very new.

MADAME ARCATI: Daphne is really more attached to Irving Berlin than anybody else. She likes a tune she can hum. Ah, here's one—'Always'.

CHARLES: (*half jumping up again*) 'Always!'

RUTH: Do sit down, Charles. What *is* the matter?

CHARLES: (*subsiding*) Nothing—nothing at all.

MADAME ARCATI: The light switch is by the door?

RUTH: Yes, all except the small one on the desk, and the gramophone.

MADAME ARCATI: Very well, I understand.

RUTH: Charles, do keep still.

MRS. BRADMAN: Fingers touching, George. Remember what Madame Arcati said.

MADAME ARCATI: Now there are one or two things that I should like to explain; so will you all listen attentively?

RUTH: Of course.

MADAME ARCATI: Presently, when the music begins, I am going to switch out the lights. I may then either walk about the room for a little or lie down flat. In due course, I shall draw up this dear little stool and join you at the table. I shall place myself between you and your wife, Mr. Condomine, and rest my hands lightly upon yours. I must ask you not to address me or move or do anything in the least distracting. Is that quite, quite clear?

CHARLES: Perfectly.

MADAME ARCATI: Of course, I cannot guarantee that anything will happen at all. Daphne may be unavailable. She had a head cold very recently, and was rather under the weather. poor child. On the other hand, a great many things might occur. One of you might have an emanation, for instance; or we might contact a poltergeist, which would be extremely destructive and noisy.

RUTH: (*anxiously*) In what way destructive?

MADAME ARCATI: They throw things, you know.

RUTH: No, I didn't know.

MADAME ARCATI: But we must cross that bridge when we come to it, mustn't we?

CHARLES: Certainly—by all means.

MADAME ARCATI: Fortunately an Elemental at this time of year is most unlikely.

RUTH: What do Elementals do?

MADAME ARCATI: Oh, my dear, one can never tell. They're dreadfully unpredictable. Usually they take the form of a very cold wind.

MRS. BRADMAN: I don't think I shall like that.

MADAME ARCATI: Occasionally reaching almost hurricane velocity.

RUTH: You don't think it would be a good idea to take the more breakable ornaments off the mantelpiece before we start?

MADAME ARCATI: (*indulgently*) That really is not necessary, Mrs. Condomine. I assure you I have my own methods of dealing with Elementals.

RUTH: I'm so glad.

MADAME ARCATI: Now then; are you ready to empty your minds?

BRADMAN: Do you mean we're to try to think of nothing?

MADAME ARCATI: Absolutely nothing, Dr. Bradman. Concentrate on a space or a nondescript colour. That's really the best way.

BRADMAN: I'll do my damndest.

MADAME ARCATI: Good work!—I will now start the music.

Madame Arcati goes to the gramophone, puts on the record of 'Always', and begins to walk about the room; occasionally she moves into an abortive little dance step. Then with sudden speed, she runs across the room and switches off the lights.

MADAME ARCATI: Lights!

MRS. BRADMAN: Oh dear!

MADAME ARCATI: Quiet—please!

In the gloom Madame Arcati, after wandering about a little, brings the stool from under the piano to between Ruth and Charles and sits at the table. The gramophone record comes to an end. There is dead silence.

MADAME ARCATI: Is there anyone there? . . . (*A long pause.*) . . . Is there anyone there? . . . (*Another long pause.*) . . . One rap for yes . . . two raps for no. Now then . . . is there anyone there?

After a shorter pause, the table gives a little bump.

MRS. BRADMAN: (*involuntarily*) Oh!

MADAME ARCATI: Sshhh! . . . Is that you Daphne? (*The table gives a louder bump.*) Is your cold better, dear? (*The table gives two loud bumps, very quickly.*) Oh, I'm so sorry. Are you doing anything for it? (*The table bumps several times.*) I'm afraid she's rather fretful . . . (*There is a silence.*) Is there anyone there who wishes to speak to anyone here? (*After a pause the table gives one bump.*) Ah! Now we're getting somewhere . . . No, Daphne, don't do that, dear, you're hurting me . . . Daphne, dear, please . . . Oh, oh, oh! . . . be good, there's a dear child . . . You say there is someone there who wishes to speak to someone here? (*One bump.*) Is it me? (*Two sharp bumps.*) Is it Dr. Bradman? (*Two bumps.*) Is it Mrs. Bradman? (*Two bumps.*) Is it Mrs. Condomine? (*Several very loud bumps, which continue until Madame Arcati shouts it down.*) Stop it! Behave yourself! Is it Mr. Condomine? (*There is dead silence for a minute, and then a very loud single bump.*) There's someone who wishes to speak to you, Mr. Condomine.

CHARLES: Tell them to leave a message.

The table bangs about loudly.

MADAME ARCATI: I really must ask you not to be flippant, Mr. Condomine.

RUTH: Charles, how can you be so idiotic? You'll spoil everything.

CHARLES: I'm sorry; it slipped out.

MADAME ARCATI: Do you know anybody who has passed over recently?

CHARLES: Not recently, except my cousin in the Civil Service, and he wouldn't be likely to want to communicate with me. We haven't spoken for years.

MADAME ARCATI: (*hysterically*) Are you Mr. Condomine's cousin in the Civil Service? (*The table bumps violently several times.*) I'm afraid we've drawn a blank. Can't you think of anyone else? Rack your brains.

RUTH: (*helpfully*) It might be old Mrs. Plummett, you know. She died on Whit Monday.

CHARLES: I can't imagine why old Mrs. Plummett should wish to talk to me. We had very little in common.

RUTH: It's worth trying, anyhow.

MADAME ARCATI: Are you old Mrs. Plummett?

The table remains still.

RUTH: She was very deaf. Perhaps you'd better shout.

MADAME ARCATI: (*shouting*) Are you old Mrs. Plummett? (*Nothing happens.*) There's nobody there at all.

MRS. BRADMAN: How disappointing; just as we were getting on so nicely.

BRADMAN: Violet, be quiet.

MADAME ARCATI: (*rising*) Well, I'm afraid there's nothing for it but for me to go into a trance. I had hoped to avoid it because it's so exhausting—however what must be must be. Excuse me a moment while I start the gramophone again.

CHARLES: (*in a strained voice*) Not 'Always'. Don't play 'Always'—

RUTH: Why ever not, Charles? Don't be absurd.

MADAME ARCATI: (*gently*) I'm afraid I must. It would be imprudent to change horses in midstream, if you know what I mean. (*She restarts the gramophone.*)

CHARLES: Have it your own way.

Madame Arcati starts to moan and comes back slowly to the stool and sits. Then in the darkness a child's voice is heard reciting rather breathlessly: 'Little Tommy Tucker'.

BRADMAN: That would be Daphne. She ought to have had her adenoids out.

MRS. BRADMAN: George— please.

Madame Arcati suddenly gives a loud scream and falls off the stool on to the floor.

CHARLES: Good God!

RUTH: Keep still, Charles . . .

Charles subsides. Everyone sits in silence for a moment, then the table starts bouncing about.

MRS. BRADMAN: It's trying to get away. I can't hold it.

RUTH: Press down hard.

The table falls over with a crash.

RUTH: There now!

MRS. BRADMAN: Ought we to pick it up or leave it where it is?

BRADMAN: How the hell do I know?

MRS. BRADMAN: There's no need to snap at me.

ELVIRA: (*off-stage*; *a perfectly strange and very charming voice*) Leave it where it is.

CHARLES: Who said that?

RUTH: Who said what?

CHARLES: Somebody said 'Leave it where it is'.

RUTH: Nonsense, dear.

CHARLES: I heard it distinctly.

RUTH: Well, nobody else did—did they?

MRS. BRADMAN: I never heard a sound.

CHARLES: It was you, Ruth. You're playing tricks.

RUTH: I'm not doing anything of the sort. I haven't uttered.

There is another pause, and then the voice says:

ELVIRA: (*off-stage*) Good evening, Charles.

CHARLES: (*very agitated*) Ventriloquism—that's what it is—ventriloquism.

RUTH: (irritably) What is the matter with you?

CHARLES: You must have heard that. One of you must have heard that!

RUTH: Heard *what*?

CHARLES: You mean to sit there solemnly and tell me that you none of you heard anything at all?

BRADMAN: I certainly didn't.

MRS. BRADMAN: Neither did I. I wish I had. I should love to hear something.

RUTH: It's you who are playing the tricks, Charles. You're acting to try to frighten us.

CHARLES: (*breathlessly*) I'm not. I swear I'm not.

ELVIRA: (*off-stage*) It's difficult to think what to say after seven years, but I suppose good evening is as good as anything else.

CHARLES: (*intensely*) Who are you?

ELVIRA: (*as before*) Elvira, of course—don't be so silly.

CHARLES: I can't bear this for another minute. . . (*He rises violently.*) Get up everybody—the entertainment's over.

Charles rushes across the room and switches on the lights. All the others rise. Madame Arcati is on the floor, her head towards the audience and her feet on the stool.

RUTH: Oh, Charles, how tiresome of you. Just as we were beginning to enjoy ourselves.

CHARLES: Never again—that's all I can say. Never, never again as long as I live.

RUTH: What on earth's the matter with you?

CHARLES: Nothing's the matter with me. I'm just sick of the whole business, that's all.

BRADMAN: Did you hear anything that we didn't hear really?

CHARLES: (*with a forced laugh*) Of course not—I was only pretending.

RUTH: I know you were.

MRS. BRADMAN: Oh dear—look at Madame Arcati!

Madame Arcati is still lying on the floor with her feet upon the stool from which she fell. She is obviously quite unconscious.

RUTH: What are we to do with her?

CHARLES: Bring her round—bring her round as soon as possible.

BRADMAN: (*going over and kneeling beside her*) I think we'd better leave her alone.

RUTH: But she might stay like that for hours.

BRADMAN: (*after feeling her pulse and examining her eye*) She's out all right.

CHARLES: (*almost hysterically*) Bring her round! It's dangerous to leave her like that.

RUTH: Really, Charles, you are behaving most peculiarly.

CHARLES: (*shaking Madame Arcati violently*) Wake up, Madame Arcati! Wake up! It's time to go home!

BRADMAN: Here—go easy, old man!

CHARLES: Get some brandy—give her some brandy, lift her into the chair—help me Bradman!

Ruth goes to the drinks table and pours out some brandy. Charles and Dr. Bradman lift Madame Arcati and put her in an armchair.

CHARLES: (*leaning over her*) Wake *up*, Madame Arcati! Little Tommy Tucker, Madame Arcati!

RUTH: (*bringing the brandy*) Here's the brandy.

Madame Arcati gives a slight moan and a shiver.

CHARLES: (*forcing some brandy between her lips*) Wake up!

Madame Arcati gives a prolonged shiver and chokes slightly over the brandy.

MRS. BRADMAN: She's coming round.

RUTH: Be careful, Charles, you're spilling it all down her dress.

MADAME ARCATI: (*opening her eyes*) Well, that's that.

RUTH: (*solicitously*) Are you all right?

MADAME ARCATI: Certainly I am. Never felt better in my life.

CHARLES: Would you like some more brandy?

MADAME ARCATI: So that's the funny taste in my mouth. Well really! Fancy allowing them to give me brandy, Dr. Bradman. You ought to have known better—brandy on top of a trance might have been catastrophic. Take it away please. I probably shan't sleep a wink tonight as it is.

CHARLES: I know I shan't.

RUTH: Why on earth not?

CHARLES: The whole experience has unhinged me.

MADAME ARCATI: Well what happened? Was it satisfactory?

RUTH: Nothing much happened, Madame Arcati, after you went off.

MADAME ARCATI: Something happened all right, I can feel it— (*She sniffs.*) No poltergeist, at any rate—that's a good thing. Any apparitions?

BRADMAN: Not a thing.

MADAME ARCATI: No ectoplasm?

RUTH: I'm not quite sure what that is, but I don't think so.

MADAME ARCATI: Very curious. I feel as though something tremendous had taken place.

RUTH: Charles pretended he heard a voice in order to frighten us.

CHARLES: It was only a joke.

MADAME ARCATI: A very poor one, if I may say so. Nevertheless, I am prepared to swear that there is someone else psychic in this room apart from myself.

RUTH: I don't see how there can be really, Madame Arcati.

MADAME ARCATI: I do hope I haven't gone and released something. However, we are bound to find out within a day or two. If any manifestation should occur or you hear any unexpected noises, you might let me know at once.

RUTH: Of course we will. We'll telephone immediately.

MADAME ARCATI: I think I really must be on my way now.

RUTH: Wouldn't you like anything before you go?

MADAME ARCATI: No, thank you. I have some Ovaltine all ready in a saucepan at home; it only needs hotting up.

BRADMAN: Wouldn't you like to leave your bicycle here and let us drive you?

MRS. BRADMAN: I honestly do think you should, Madame Arcati. After that trance and everything you can't be feeling quite yourself.

MADAME ARCATI: Nonsense, my dear, I'm as fit as a fiddle. Always feel capital after a trance—rejuvenates me. Good night, Mrs. Condomine.

RUTH: It was awfully sweet of you to take so much trouble.

MADAME ARCATI: I'm so sorry so little occurred. It's that cold of Daphne's I expect. You know what children are when they have anything wrong with them. We must try again some other evening.

RUTH: That would be lovely.

MADAME ARCATI: (*shaking hands with Mrs. Bradman*) Good night Mrs. Bradman.

MRS. BRADMAN: It was thrilling, it really was. I felt the table absolutely shaking under my hands.

Madame Arcati crosses to Dr. Bradman and shakes hands.

MADAME ARCATI: Good night, doctor.

BRADMAN: Congratulations, Madame Arcati.

MADAME ARCATI: I am fully aware of the irony in your voice, Dr. Bradman. As a matter of fact you'd be an admirable subject for telepathic hypnosis. A great chum of mine is an expert. I should like her to look you over.

BRADMAN: I'm sure I should be charmed.

MADAME ARCATI: Good night everyone. Next time we must really put our backs into it!

With a comprehensive smile and a wave of the hand, Madame Arcati goes out, followed by Charles. Ruth sinks down into the sofa, laughing helplessly.

RUTH: Oh dear! . . . oh dear!

MRS. BRADMAN: (*beginning to laugh too*) Be careful, Mrs. Condomine; she might hear you.

RUTH: I can't help it. I really can't. I've been holding this in for ages.

MRS. BRADMAN: She certainly put you in your place, George, and serve you right.

RUTH: She's raving mad, of course; mad as a hatter.

MRS. BRADMAN: But do you think she really *believes*?

BRADMAN: Of course not. The whole thing's a put-up job. I must say, though, she shoots a more original line than they generally do.

RUTH: I should think that she's probably half convinced herself by now.

BRADMAN: Possibly. The trance was genuine enough; but that, of course, is easily accounted for.

RUTH: Hysteria?

BRADMAN: Yes—a form of hysteria, I should imagine.

MRS. BRADMAN: I do hope Mr. Condomine got all the atmosphere he wanted for his book.

RUTH: He might have got a great deal more if he hadn't spoiled everything by showing off . . . I'm really very cross with him.

At this moment Elvira comes in through the french windows. She is charmingly dressed in a sort of négligée. Everything about her is grey; hair, skin, dress, hands, so we must accept the fact that she is not quite of this world. She passes between Dr. and Mrs. Bradman and Ruth while they are talking. None of them sees her. She moves to the fireplace and regards them with interest, a slight smile on her face.

RUTH: I suddenly felt a draught—there must be a window open.

BRADMAN: (*looking*) No—they're shut.

MRS. BRADMAN: (*laughing*) Perhaps it was one of those what you may call 'ems that Madame Arcati was talking about.

BRADMAN: Elementals.

RUTH: (*also laughing again*) Oh no, it couldn't be. She distinctly said it was the wrong time of year for Elementals.

CHARLES: (*coming in*) Well, the old girl's gone pedalling off down the drive at a hell of a speed. We had a bit of trouble lighting her lamp.

MRS. BRADMAN: Poor thing.

CHARLES: I've got a theory about her, you know. I believe she is completely sincere.

RUTH: Charles! How could she be?

CHARLES: Wouldn't it be possible, doctor? Some form of self-hypnotism?

BRADMAN: It might be. As I was explaining to your wife just now, there are certain types of hysterical subjects. . .

MRS. BRADMAN: George, dear, it's getting terribly late, we really must go home. You have to get up so early in the morning.

BRADMAN: You see? The moment I begin to talk about anything that really interests me, my wife interrupts me.

MRS. BRADMAN: You know I'm right, darling—it's past eleven.

BRADMAN: I'll do a little reading up on the whole business; just for the fun of it.

CHARLES: You must have a drink before you go.

BRADMAN: No, really, thank you. Violet's quite right, I'm afraid. I have got to get up abominably early tomorrow. I have a patient being operated on in Canterbury.

MRS. BRADMAN: (to Ruth) It has been a thrilling evening. I shall never forget it. It was sweet of you to include us.

BRADMAN: Good night, Mrs. Condomine. Thank you so much.

CHARLES: You're sure about the drink?

BRADMAN: Quite sure, thanks.

RUTH: We'll let you know if we find any poltergeists whirling about.

BRADMAN: I should never forgive you if you didn't.

MRS. BRADMAN: Come along, darling.

The Bradmans go out, followed by Charles. Ruth leans over Elvira and gets a cigarette and lights it. Charles comes back into the room.

RUTH: Well, darling?

CHARLES: (*absently*) Well?

RUTH: Would you say the evening had been profitable?

CHARLES: Yes—I suppose so.

RUTH: I must say it was extremely funny at moments.

CHARLES: Yes—it certainly was.

RUTH: What's the matter?

CHARLES: The matter?

RUTH: Yes. You seem odd, somehow. Do you feel quite well?

CHARLES: Perfectly. I think I'll have a drink. Do you want one?

RUTH: No, thank you, dear.

CHARLES: (*moving to the drinks table and pouring out a whisky and soda*) It's rather chilly in this room.

RUTH: Come over by the fire.

CHARLES: I don't think I'll make any notes tonight. I'll start fresh in the morning. (*He turns, glass in hand. He sees Elvira for the first time and drops the glass on the floor.*) My God!

RUTH: Charles!

ELVIRA: That was very clumsy, Charles dear.

CHARLES: Elvira!—then it's true—it was you!

ELVIRA: Of course it was.

RUTH: Charles—darling Charles—what are you talking about?

CHARLES: (*to Elvira*) Are you a ghost?

ELVIRA: I suppose I must be. It's all very confusing.

RUTH: Charles—what do you keep looking over there for? Look at me? What's happened?

CHARLES: Don't you see?

RUTH: See what?

CHARLES: Elvira.

RUTH: (*staring at him incredulously*) Elvira! !

CHARLES: (*with an effort at social grace*) Yes. Elvira dear, this is Ruth. Ruth, this is Elvira.

RUTH: (*with forced calmness, trying to take his arm*) Come and sit down, darling.

CHARLES: Do you mean to say you can't see her?

RUTH: Listen, Charles—you just sit down quietly by the fire and I'll mix you another drink. Don't worry about the mess on the carpet, Edith can clean it up in the morning.

CHARLES: But you must be able to see her—she's there—look—right in front of you—there!

RUTH: Are you mad? What's happened to you?

CHARLES: You can't see her?

RUTH: If this is a joke, dear, it's gone quite far enough. Sit down for God's sake, and don't be idiotic.

CHARLES: (*clutching his head*) What am I to do! What the hell am I to do!

ELVIRA: I think you might at least be a little more pleased to see me. After all, you conjured me up.

CHARLES: I didn't do any such thing.

ELVIRA: Nonsense; of course you did. That awful child with the cold came and told me you wanted to see me urgently.

CHARLES: It was all a mistake, a horrible mistake.

RUTH: Stop talking like that, Charles. As I told you before the joke's gone far enough.

CHARLES: I've gone mad, that's what it is, I've just gone raving mad.

RUTH: (*pouring out some brandy and bringing it to Charles*) Here, drink this.

CHARLES: (*mechanically—taking it*) This is appalling!

RUTH: Relax.

CHARLES: How can I relax? I shall never be able to relax again as long as I live.

RUTH: Drink some brandy.

CHARLES: (*drinking it at a gulp*) There! Now are you satisfied?

RUTH: Now sit down.

CHARLES: Why are you so anxious for me to sit down? What good will that do?

RUTH: I want you to relax. You can't relax standing up.

ELVIRA: African natives can. They can stand on one leg for hours.

CHARLES: I don't happen to be an African native.

RUTH: You don't happen to be a *what*?

CHARLES: (*savagely*) An African native.

RUTH: What's that got to do with it?

CHARLES: It doesn't matter, Ruth; really it doesn't matter. (*He sits.*) We'll say no more about it. See, I've sat down.

RUTH: Would you like some more brandy?

CHARLES: Yes, please.

Ruth goes to the drinks table with the glass.

ELVIRA: Very unwise. You always had a weak head.

CHARLES: I could drink you under the table.

RUTH: There's no need to be aggressive, Charles. I'm doing my best to help you.

CHARLES: I'm sorry.

RUTH: (*coming to Charles with the brandy*) Here, drink this; and then we'll go to bed.

ELVIRA: Get rid of her, Charles; then we can talk in peace.

CHARLES: That's a thoroughly immoral suggestion. You ought to be ashamed of yourself.

RUTH: What is there immoral in that?

CHARLES: I wasn't talking to you.

RUTH: Who were you talking to, then?

CHARLES: Elvira, of course.

RUTH: To hell with Elvira!

ELVIRA: There now—she's getting cross.

CHARLES: I don't blame her.

RUTH: What don't you blame her for?

CHARLES: Oh, God!

RUTH: Now, look here, Charles, I gather you've got some sort of plan behind all this. I'm not quite a fool. I suspected you when we were doing that idiotic seance.

CHARLES: Don't be so silly. What plan could I have?

RUTH: I don't know. It's probably something to do with the characters in your book—how they, or one of them, would react to a certain situation. I refuse to be used as a guinea-pig unless I'm warned beforehand what it's all about.

CHARLES: Elvira is here, Ruth—she's standing a few yards away from you.

RUTH: (*sarcastically*) Yes, dear, I can see her distinctly—under the piano with a zebra!

CHARLES: But Ruth—

RUTH: I am not going to stay here arguing any longer.

ELVIRA: Hurray!

CHARLES: Shut up!

RUTH: (*incensed*) How dare you to speak to me like that?

CHARLES: Listen, Ruth. Please listen—

RUTH: I will not listen to any more of this nonsense. I am going up to bed now; I'll leave you to turn out the lights. I shan't be asleep. I'm too upset. So you can come in and say good night to me if you feel like it.

ELVIRA: That's big of her, I must say.

CHARLES: Be quiet. You're behaving like a guttersnipe.

RUTH: (*icily*) That is all I have to say. Good night, Charles. *Ruth walks swiftly out of the room without looking at Charles again.*

CHARLES: (*following her to the door*) Ruth—

ELVIRA: That was one of the most enjoyable half-hours I have ever spent.

CHARLES: Oh, Elvira—how could you!

ELVIRA: Poor Ruth!

CHARLES: (*staring at her*) This is obviously an hallucination, isn't it?

ELVIRA: I'm afraid I don't know the technical term for it.

CHARLES: What am I to do?

ELVIRA: What Ruth suggested—relax.

CHARLES: Where have you come from?

ELVIRA: Do you know, it's very peculiar, but I've sort of forgotten.

CHARLES: Are you here indefinitely?

ELVIRA: I don't know that either.

CHARLES: Oh, my God!

ELVIRA: Why? Would you hate it so much if I was?

CHARLES: Well, you must admit it would be embarrassing.

ELVIRA: I don't see why, really. It's all a question of adjusting yourself. Anyhow, I think it's horrid of you to be so unwelcoming and disagreeable.

CHARLES: Now look here, Elvira—

ELVIRA: (*near tears*) I do. I think you're mean.

CHARLES: Try to see my point, dear. I've been married to Ruth for five years, and you've been dead for seven . . .

ELVIRA: Not dead, Charles. 'Passed over.' It's considered vulgar to say 'dead' where I come from.

CHARLES: Passed over, then.

ELVIRA: At any rate, now that I'm here, the least you can do is to make a pretence of being amiable about it.

CHARLES: Of course, my dear, I'm delighted in one way.

ELVIRA: I don't believe you love me any more.

CHARLES: I shall always love the memory of you.

ELVIRA: You mustn't think me unreasonable, but I really am a little hurt. You called me back; and at great inconvenience I came—and you've been thoroughly churlish ever since I arrived.

CHARLES: (*gently*) Believe me, Elvira, I most emphatically did not send for you. There's been some mistake.

ELVIRA: (*irritably*) Well, somebody did—and that child said it was you. I remember I was playing backgammon with a very sweet old Oriental gentleman, I think his name was Genghiz Khan, and I'd just thrown double sixes, and then the child paged me and the next thing I knew I was in this room. Perhaps it was your subconscious . . .

CHARLES: You must find out whether you are going to stay or not, and we can make arrangements accordingly.

ELVIRA: I don't see how I can.

CHARLES: Well, try to think. Isn't there someone you know, that you can get in touch with over there—on the other side, or whatever it's called—who could advise you?

ELVIRA: I can't think—it seems so far away—as though I'd dreamed it . . .

CHARLES: You must know somebody else besides Genghiz Khan.

ELVIRA: Oh, Charles . . .

CHARLES: What is it?

ELVIRA: I want to cry, but I don't think I'm able to.

CHARLES: What do you want to cry for?

ELVIRA: It's seeing you again—and you being so irascible, like you always used to be.

CHARLES: I don't mean to be irascible, Elvira.

ELVIRA: Darling—I don't mind really—I never did.

CHARLES: Is it cold—being a ghost?

ELVIRA: No—I don't think so.

CHARLES: What happens if I touch you?

ELVIRA: I doubt if you can. Do you want to?

CHARLES: Oh, Elvira . . . (*He buries his face in his hands.*)

ELVIRA: What is it, darling?

CHARLES: I really do feel strange, seeing you again.

ELVIRA: That's better.

CHARLES: (*looking up*) What's better?

ELVIRA: Your voice was kinder.

CHARLES: Was I ever unkind to you when you were alive?

ELVIRA: Often.

CHARLES: Oh, how can you! I'm sure that's an exaggeration.

ELVIRA: Not at all. You were an absolute pig that time we went to Cornwall and stayed in that awful hotel. You hit me with a billiard cue.

CHARLES: Only very, very gently.

ELVIRA: I loved you very much.

CHARLES: I loved you too . . . (*He puts out his hand to her and then draws it away.*) No, I can't touch you. Isn't that horrible?

ELVIRA: Perhaps it's as well if I'm going to stay for any length of time. (*She sits on the arm of his chair.*)

CHARLES: I suppose I shall wake up eventually . . . but I feel strangely peaceful now.

ELVIRA: That's right. Put your head back.

CHARLES: (*doing so*) Like that?

ELVIRA. (*stroking his hair*) Can you feel anything?

CHARLES: Only a very little breeze through my hair . . .

ELVIRA: Well, that's better than nothing.

CHARLES: (*drowsily*) I suppose if I'm really out of my mind they'll put me in an asylum.

ELVIRA: Don't worry about that—just relax.

CHARLES: (*very drowsily indeed*) Poor Ruth.

ELVIRA: (*gently and sweetly*) To hell with Ruth.

Verse Plays of the Twentieth Century

THE FAMILY REUNION

(Part I, Scene I)

by

T. S. Eliot

CHARACTERS

AMY, DOWAGER LADY MONCHENSEY.
IVY
VIOLET } *her. younger, unmarried sisters.*
AGATHA
COLONEL THE HON. GERALD PIPER } *brothers of her deceased*
THE HON. CHARLES PIPER } *husband.*
MARY, *daughter of a deceased cousin of Amy.*
DENMAN, *a parlourmaid.*
HARRY, LORD MONCHENSEY, *Amy's eldest son.*
DOWNING, *his servant and chauffeur.*

THE AUTHOR

T. S. Eliot was born in America in 1888, but lived and worked for so long in England that most people are unaware of his American background. He was, without doubt, one of the major poets of our time, and it is, therefore, a matter of some importance that he turned his hand to the theatre. His first play, *Murder in the Cathedral*, is his best known. It was written in 1935 for the Chapter House of Canterbury Cathedral, but afterwards was immensely successful in the commercial theatre. Eliot was not satisfied, however, as he was determined to try to restore poetry to the modern theatre,

78

writing plays with contemporary themes and set in the contemporary world. In 1939 he put his theories to the test with *The Family Reunion*, an extract from which is included here. It was a commercial failure, although it has been revived since World War II with some success, but Eliot was not to be deterred. During the forties and fifties, he wrote *The Cocktail Party* and *The Confidential Clerk*, but found that in order to make verse more acceptable in a modern setting, he had to make it sound more and more like prose. It could be claimed that *The Confidential Clerk* is hardly in verse at all, and the twentieth century still awaits its great poetic dramatist who can catch its mood as Shakespeare did in the Elizabethan Age.

THE PLAY
The Family Reunion opens with Amy, Dowager Lady Monchensey, surrounded by her sisters and the brothers of her deceased husband, awaiting the arrival of her sons Harry, Arthur and John. It is her birthday and the family always assembles to celebrate it, but this is a special occasion because Harry, the present Lord Monchensey, has not seen his family for eight years. Since his marriage, he has lived out of England as his family (in particular, his mother) have not approved of his wife. She is now dead, having fallen overboard from a passenger liner, and Harry is coming home for the family reunion. It is hardly a joyous occasion. Harry tells his family that he murdered his wife by pushing her overboard, and, from the others' point of view, his mind seems so disordered that they doubt his sanity.

At no point in the play is it made clear whether Harry murdered his wife or not, and from Eliot's point of view it hardly matters one way or the other. The family is cursed, and Harry has to work

out the curse. (It should be noted that Eliot has used the Greek story of Orestes as the basis of his play.)[1] Harry is pursued by the Eumenides or Furies, legendary figures seen only by the guilty, and even in his childhood home he is unable to escape them. But Eliot's attitude is a Christian one. Harry finds peace when he learns that the Eumenides are not vengeful demons, but agents of God's love, and towards the end of the play he leaves, renouncing his title, to learn the lesson of God's love 'somewhere on the other side of despair'.

The scene included here is the opening scene of the play. It shows clearly Eliot's attempt to write a 'drawing-room play' using poetic dialogue, and it even includes some of the elements of a mystery play. An interesting device is the use of the uncles and aunts as a chorus of voices, the implication being that, when speaking together, they are an expression of common family feeling. Eliot himself has stated that this device was a failure, but his judgement is open to question as in many productions it has succeeded admirably.

[1] Orestes was the son of Agamemnon, King of Mycenae and conqueror of Troy. On his return from the Trojan War, Agamemnon was killed by his wife, Clytemnestra, who was killed herself, in turn, by Orestes, her own son, according to the old law of vendetta. Orestes was in an unenviable position: if he killed his mother he was guilty of matricide; if he did not kill her, he was leaving his father unavenged. After his dreadful deed, Orestes was pursued by the Furies, or Eumenides, until by suffering he expiated his sin and removed the curse on his family.

THE FAMILY REUNION

Part I, Scene I

The scene is the drawing-room of Lady Monchensey's house, after tea, on an afternoon in late March.
Amy, Ivy, Violet, Agatha, Gerald, Charles and Mary are sitting in the room. Denman enters to draw the curtains.

AMY: Not yet! I will ring for you. It is still quite light.
I have nothing to do but watch the days draw out,
Now that I sit in the house from October to June,
And the swallow comes too soon and the spring will be over
And the cuckoo will be gone before I am out again.
O Sun, that was once so warm, O light that was taken for granted
When I was young and strong, and sun and light unsought for
And the night unfeared and the day expected
And clocks could be trusted, tomorrow assured
And time would not stop in the dark!
Put on the lights. But leave the curtains undrawn.
Make up the fire. Will the spring never come? I am cold.

AGATHA: Wishwood was always a cold place, Amy.

IVY: I have always told Amy she should go south in the winter.
Were I in Amy's position, I would go south in the winter.
I would follow the sun, not wait for the sun to come here.
I would go south in the winter, if I could afford it,
Not freeze, as I do, in Bayswater, by a gas fire counting shillings.

VIOLET: Go south! to the English circulating libraries,
To the military widows and the English chaplains,
To the chilly deck-chair and the strong cold tea—
The strong cold stewed bad Indian tea.

CHARLES: That's not Amy's style at all. We are country-bred
people.
Amy has been too long used to our ways
Living with horses and dogs and guns
Ever to want to leave England in the winter.
But a single man like me is better off in London:

81

A man can be very cosy at his club
Even in an English winter.
GERALD: Well, as for me,
I'd just as soon be a subaltern again
To be back in the East. An incomparable climate
For a man who can exercise a little common prudence;
And your servants look after you very much better.
AMY: My servants are perfectly competent, Gerald.
I can still see to that.
VIOLET: Well, as for me,
I would never go south, no, definitely never,
Even could I do it as well as Amy:
England's bad enough, I would never go south,
Simply to see the vulgarest people—
You can keep out of their way at home;
People with money from heaven knows where—
GERALD: Dividends from aeroplane shares.
VIOLET: They bathe all day and they dance all night
In the absolute *minimum* of clothes.
CHARLES: It's the cocktail-drinking does the harm:
There's nothing on earth so bad for the young.
All that a civilized person needs
Is a glass of dry sherry or two before dinner.
The modern young people don't know what they're drinking,
Modern young people don't care what they're eating;
They've lost their sense of taste and smell
Because of their cocktails and cigarettes.
        (*Enter Denman with sherry and whisky. Charles takes sherry
        and Gerald whisky.*)
That's what it comes to.
        (*Lights a cigarette.*)
IVY: The younger generation
Are undoubtedly decadent.
CHARLES: The younger generation
Are not what we were. Haven't the stamina,
Haven't the sense of responsibility.
GERALD: You're being very hard on the younger generation.
I don't come across them very much now, myself;
But I must say I've met some very decent specimens
And some first-class shots—better than you were,

Charles, as I remember. Besides you've got to make allowances:
We haven't left them such an easy world to live in.
Let the younger generation speak for itself:
It's Mary's generation. What does she think about it?

MARY: Really, Cousin Gerald, if you want information
About the younger generation, you must ask someone else.
I'm afraid that I don't deserve the compliment:
I don't belong to any generation.

(*Exit.*)

VIOLET: Really, Gerald, I must say you're very tactless,
And I think Charles might have been more considerate.

GERALD: I'm very sorry: but why was she upset?
I only meant to draw her into the conversation.

CHARLES: She's a nice girl; but it's a difficult age for her.
I suppose she must be getting on for thirty?
She ought to be married, that's what it is.

AMY: So she should have been, if things had gone as I intended.
Harry's return does not make things easy for her
At the moment: but life may still go right.
Meanwhile, let us drop the subject. The less said the better.

GERALD: That reminds me, Amy.
When are the boys all due to arrive?

AMY: I do not want the clock to stop in the dark.
If you want to know why I never leave Wishwood
That is the reason. I keep Wishwood alive
To keep the family alive, to keep them together,
To keep me alive, and I live to keep them.
You none of you understand how old you are
And death will come to you as mild surprise,
A momentary shudder is a vacant room.
Only Agatha seems to discover some meaning in death
Which I cannot find.
—I am only certain of Arthur and John,
Arthur in London, John in Leicestershire:
They should both be here in good time for dinner.
Harry telephoned to me from Marseilles,
He would come by air to Paris, and so to London,
And hoped to arrive in the course of the evening.

VIOLET: Harry was always the most likely to be late.

AMY: This time, it will not be his fault.
We are very lucky to have Harry at all.

IVY: And when will you have your birthday cake, Amy,
And open your presents?

AMY: After dinner:
That is the best time.

IVY: It is the first time
You have not had your cake and your presents at tea.

AMY: This is a very particular occasion
As you ought to know. It will be the first time
For eight years that we have all been together.

AGATHA: It is going to be rather painful for Harry
After eight years and all that has happened
To come back to Wishwood.

GERALD: Why, painful?

VIOLET: Gerald! you know what Agatha means.

AGATHA: I mean painful, because everything is irrevocable,
Because the past is irremediable,
Because the future can only be built
Upon the real past. Wandering in the tropics
Or against the painted scene of the Mediterranean,
Harry must often have remembered Wishwood—
The nursery tea, the school holiday,
The daring feats on the old pony,
And thought to creep back through the little door.
He will find a new Wishwood. Adaptation is hard.

AMY: Nothing is changed, Agatha, at Wishwood.
Everything is kept as it was when he left it,
Except the old pony, and the mongrel setter
Which I had to have destroyed.
Nothing has been changed. I have seen to that.

AGATHA: Yes. I mean that at Wishwood he will find another
    Harry.
The man who returns will have to meet
The boy who left. Round by the stables,
In the coach-house, in the orchard,
In the plantation, down the corridor
That led to the nursery, round the corner
Of the new wing, he will have to face him—
And it will not be a very *jolly* corner.

When the loop in time comes—and it does not come for everybody—
The hidden is revealed, and the spectres show themselves.
  GERALD: I don't in the least know what you're talking about.
You seem to be wanting to give us all the hump.
I must say, this isn't cheerful for Amy's birthday
Or for Harry's homecoming. Make him feel at home, I say!
Make him feel that what has happened doesn't matter.
He's taken his medicine, I've no doubt.
Let him marry again and carry on at Wishwood.
  AMY: Thank you, Gerald. Though Agatha means
As a rule, a good deal more than she cares to betray,
I am bound to say that I agree with you.
  CHARLES: I never wrote to him when he lost his wife—
That was just about a year ago, wasn't it?
Do you think that I ought to mention it now?
It seems to me too late.
  AMY: Much too late.
If he wants to talk about it, that's another matter;
But I don't believe he will. He will wish to forget it.
I do not mince matters in front of the family:
You can call it nothing but a blessed relief.
  VIOLET: *I* call it providential.
  IVY: Yet it must have been shocking,
Especially to lose anybody in *that* way—
Swept off the deck in the middle of a storm,
And never to recover the body.
  CHARLES: 'Well-known Peeress Vanishes from Liner.'
  GERALD: Yes, it's odd to think of her as permanently *missing*.
  VIOLET: Had she been drinking?
  AMY: I would never ask him.
  IVY: These things are much better not enquired into.
She may have done it in a fit of temper.
  GERALD: I never met her.
  AMY: I am very glad you did not.
·I am very glad that none of you ever met her.
It will make the situation very much easier
And is why I was so anxious you should all be here.
She never would have been one of the family,
She never wished to be one of the family,
She only wanted to keep him to herself

To satisfy her vanity. That's why she dragged him
All over Europe and half round the world
To expensive hotels and undesirable society
Which she could choose herself. She never wanted
Harry's relations or Harry's old friends;
She never wanted to fit herself to Harry,
But only to bring Harry down to her own level.
A restless shivering painted shadow
In life, she is less than a shadow in death.
You might as well all of you know the truth
For the sake of the future. There can be no grief
And no regret and no remorse.
I would have prevented it if I could. For the sake of the future:
Harry is to command at Wishwood
And I hope we can contrive his future happiness.
Do not discuss his absence. Please behave only
As if nothing had happened in the last eight years.

    GERALD: That will be a little difficult.

    VIOLET: Nonsense, Gerald!
You must see for yourself it's the only thing to do.

    AGATHA: Thus with most careful devotion
Thus with precise attention
To detail, interfering preparation
Of that which is already prepared
Men tighten the knot of confusion
Into perfect misunderstanding,
Reflecting a pocket-torch of observation
Upon each other's opacity
Neglecting all the admonitions
From the world around the corner
The wind's talk in the dry holly-tree
The inclination of the moon
The attraction of the dark passage
The paw under the door.

    CHORUS (IVY, VIOLET, GERALD AND CHARLES):
Why do we feel embarrassed, impatient, fretful, ill at ease,
Assembled like amateur actors who have not been assigned their
    parts?
Like amateur actors in a dream when the curtain rises, to find

themselves dressed for a different play, or having rehearsed
the wrong parts,
Waiting for the rustling in the stalls, the titter in the dress circle,
the laughter and catcalls in the gallery?

CHARLES: I might have been in St. James's Street, in a comfortable chair rather nearer the fire.

IVY: I might have been visiting Cousin Lily at Sidmouth, if I
had not had to come to this party.

GERALD: I might have been staying with Compton-Smith, down
at his place in Dorset.

VIOLET: I should have been helping Lady Bumpus, at the
Vicar's American Tea.

CHORUS: Yet we are here at Amy's command, to play an unread
part in some monstrous farce, ridiculous in some nightmare
pantomime.

AMY: What's that? I thought I saw someone pass the window.
What time is it?

CHARLES: Nearly twenty to seven.

AMY: John should be here by now, he has the shortest way to
come.

John at least, if not Arthur. Hark, there is someone coming:
Yes it must be John.

(*Enter Harry.*)

Harry!

(*Harry stops suddenly at the door and stares at the window.*)

IVY: Welcome, Harry!

GERALD: Well done!

VIOLET: Welcome home to Wishwood!

CHARLES: Why, what's the matter?

AMY: Harry, if you want the curtains drawn you should let me
ring for Denman.

HARRY: How can you sit in this blaze of light for all the world
to look at?

If you knew how you looked, when I saw you through the window!
Do you like to be stared at by eyes through a window?

AMY: You forget, Harry, that you are at Wishwood,
Not in town, where you have to close the blinds.
There is no one to see you but our servants who belong here,
And who all want to see you back, Harry.

HARRY: Look there, look there: do you see them?

GERALD: No, I don't see anyone about.

HARRY:　　　　　　　　　No, no, not there. Look there!
Can't you see them? *You* don't see them, but I see them,
And they see me. This is the first time that I have seen them.
In the Java Straits, in the Sunda Sea,
In the sweet sickly tropical night, I knew they were coming.
In Italy, from behind the nightingale's thicket,
The eyes stared at me, and corrupted that song.
Behind the palm trees in the Grand Hotel
They were always there. But I did not *see* them.
Why should they wait until I came back to Wishwood?
There were a thousand places where I might have met them!
Why here? why here?
　　　　　　　　　Many happy returns of the day, mother.
Aunt Ivy, Aunt Violet, Uncle Gerald, Uncle Charles. Agatha.

AMY: We are very glad to have you back, Harry.
Now we shall all be together for dinner.
The servants have been looking forward to your coming:
Would you like to have them in after dinner
Or wait till tomorrow? I am sure you must be tired.
You will find everybody here, and everything the same.
Mr. Bevan—you remember—wants to call tomorrow
On some legal business, a question about taxes—
But I think you would rather wait till you are rested.
Your room is all ready for you. Nothing has been changed.

HARRY: Changed? nothing changed? how can you say that
nothing is changed?
You all look so withered and young.

GERALD:　　　　　　　　We must have a ride tomorrow.
You'll find you know the country as well as ever.
There wasn't an inch of it you didn't know.
But you'll have to see about a couple of new hunters.

CHARLES: And I have a new wine merchant to recommend you;
Your cellar could do with a little attention.

IVY: And you'll have to find a successor to old Hawkins.
It's really high time the old man was pensioned.
He's let the rock garden go to rack and ruin,
And he's nearly half-blind. I've spoken to your mother
Time and time again: she's done nothing about it
Because she preferred to wait for your coming.

VIOLET: And time and time I have spoken to your mother
About the waste that goes on in the kitchen.
Mrs. Packell is too old to know what she is doing.
It really needs a man in charge of things at Wishwood.
      AMY: You see your aunts and uncles are very helpful, Harry.
I have always found them forthcoming with advice
Which I have never taken. Now it is your business.
I have only struggled to keep Wishwood going
And to make no changes before your return.
Now it's for you to manage. I am an old woman.
They can give me no further advice when I'm dead.
      IVY: Oh, dear Amy!
No one wants you to die, I'm sure!
Now that Harry's back, is the time to think of living.
      HARRY: Time and time and time, and change, no change!
You all of you try to talk as if nothing had happened,
And yet you talk of nothing else. Why not get to the point
Or if you want to pretend that I am another person—
A person that you have conspired to invent, please do so
In my absence. I shall be less embarrassing to you. Agatha?
      AGATHA: I think, Harry, that having got so far—
If you want no pretences, let us have no pretences:
And you must try at once to make us understand
And we must try to understand you.
      HARRY: But how can I explain, how can I explain to *you*?
You will understand less after I have explained it.
All that I could hope to make you understand
Is only events: not what has happened.
And people to whom nothing has ever happened
Cannot understand the unimportance of events.
      GERALD: Well, you can't say that nothing has happened to *me*.
I started as a youngster on the North-West Frontier—
Been in tight corners most of my life
And some pretty nasty messes.
      CHARLES: And there isn't much would surprise me, Harry;
Or shock me, either.
      HARRY: You are all people
To whom nothing has happened, at most a continual impact
Of external events. You have gone through life in sleep,
Never woken to the nightmare. I tell you, life would be unendurable

If you were wide awake. You do not know
The noxious smell untraceable in the drains,
Inaccessible to the plumbers, that has its hour of the night; you
    do not know
The unspoken voice of sorrow in the ancient bedroom
At three o'clock in the morning. I am not speaking
Of my own experience, but trying to give you
Comparisons in a more familiar medium. I am the old house
With the noxious smell and the sorrow before morning,
In which all past is present, all degradation
Is unredeemable. As for what happens—
Of the past you can only see what is past,
Not what is always present. That is what matters.

    AGATHA: Nevertheless, Harry, best tell us as you can:
Talk in your own language, without stopping to debate
Whether it may be too far beyond our understanding.

    HARRY: The sudden solitude in a crowded desert
In a thick smoke, many creatures moving
Without direction, for no direction
Leads anywhere but round and round in that vapour—
Without purpose, and without principle of conduct
In flickering intervals of light and darkness;
The partial anaesthesia of suffering without feeling
And partial observation of one's own automatism
While the slow stain sinks deeper through the skin
Tainting the flesh and discolouring the bone—
This is what matters, but it is unspeakable,
Untranslatable: I talk in general terms
Because the particular has no language. One thinks to escape
By violence, but one is still alone
In an over-crowded desert, jostled by ghosts.
It was only reversing the senseless direction
For a momentary rest on the burning wheel
That cloudless night in the mid-Atlantic
When I pushed her over.

    VIOLET: Pushed her?

    HARRY: You would never imagine anyone could sink so quickly.
I had always supposed, wherever I went
That she would be with me; whatever I did
That she was unkillable. It was not like that.

Everything is true in a different sense.
I expected to find her when I went back to the cabin.
Later, I became excited, I think I made enquiries;
The purser and the steward were extremely sympathetic
And the doctor was very attentive.
That night I slept heavily, alone.

    AMY: Harry!

    CHARLES: You mustn't indulge such dangerous fancies.
It's only doing harm to your mother and yourself.
Of course we know what really happened, we read it in the papers—
No need to revert to it. Remember, my boy,
I understand, your life together made it seem more horrible.
There's a lot in my own past life that presses on my chest
When I wake, as I do now, early before morning.
I understand these feelings better than you know—
But *you* have no reason to reproach yourself.
Your conscience can be clear.

    HARRY: It goes a good deal deeper
Than what people call their conscience; it is just the cancer
That eats away the self. I knew how you would take it.
First of all, you isolate the single event
As something so dreadful that it couldn't have happened,
Because you could not bear it. So you must believe
That I suffer from delusions. It is not my conscience,
Not my mind, that is diseased, but the world I have to live in.
—I lay two days in contented drowsiness;
Then I recovered. I am afraid of sleep:
A condition in which one can be caught for the last time.
And also waking. She is nearer than ever.
The contamination has reached the marrow
And *they* are always near. Here, nearer than ever.
They are very close here. I had not expected that.

    AMY: Harry, Harry, you are very tired
And overwrought. Coming so far
And making such haste, the change is too sudden for you.
You are unused to our foggy climate
And the northern country. When you see Wishwood
Again by day, all will be the same again.
I beg you to go now and rest before dinner.

Get Downing to draw you a hot bath,
And you will feel better.

AGATHA: There are certain points I do not yet understand:
They will be clear later. I am also convinced
That you only hold a fragment of the explanation.
It is only because of what you do not understand
That you feel the need to declare what you do.
There is more to understand: hold fast to that
As the way to freedom.

HARRY: I think I see what you mean,
Dimly—as you once explained the sobbing in the chimney
The evil in the dark closet, which they said was not there,
Which they explained away, but you explained them
Or at least, made me cease to be afraid of them.
I will go and have my bath.
(*Exit.*)

GERALD: God preserve us!
I never thought it would be as bad as this.

VIOLET: There is only one thing to be done:
Harry must see a doctor.

IVY: But I understand—
I have heard of such cases before—that people in his condition
Often betray the most immoderate resentment
At such a suggestion. They can be very cunning—
Their malady makes them so. They do not want to be cured
And they know what you are thinking.

CHARLES: He has probably let this notion grow in his mind,
Living among strangers, with no one to talk to.
I suspect it is simply that the wish to get rid of her
Makes him believe he did. He cannot trust his good fortune.
I believe that all he needs is someone to talk to,
To get it off his mind. I'll have a talk to him tomorrow.

AMY: Most certainly not, Charles, you are not the right person.
I prefer to believe that a few days at Wishwood
Among his own family, is all that he needs.

GERALD: Nevertheless, Amy, there's something in Violet's
suggestion.
Why not ring up Warburton, and ask him to join us?
He's an old friend of the family, it's perfectly natural
That he should be asked. He looked after all the boys

When they were children. I'll have a word with him.
He can talk to Harry, and Harry need have no suspicion.
I'd trust Warburton's opinion.

AMY: If anyone speaks to Dr. Warburton
It should be myself. What does Agatha think?

AGATHA: It seems a necessary move
In an unnecessary action,
Not for the good that it will do
But that nothing may be left undone
On the margin of the possible.

AMY: Very well.
I will ring up the doctor myself.
(*Exit.*)

CHARLES: Meanwhile, I have an idea. Why not question
Downing?
He's been with Harry ten years, he's absolutely discreet.
He was with them on the boat. He might be of use.

IVY: Charles! you don't really suppose
That he might have pushed her over?

CHARLES: In any case, I shouldn't blame Harry.
I might have done the same thing once, myself.
Nobody knows what he's likely to do
Until there's somebody he wants to get rid of.

GERALD: Even so, we don't want Downing to know
Any more than he knows already.
And even if he knew, it's very much better
That he shouldn't know that we knew it also.
Why not let sleeping dogs lie?

CHARLES: All the same, there's a question or two
(*Rings the bell.*)
That I'd like to ask Downing.
                          He shan't know why I'm asking.
(*Enter Denman.*)
Denman, where is Downing? Is he up with his Lordship?

DENMAN: He's out in the garage, Sir, with his Lordship's car.

CHARLES: Tell him I'd like to have a word with him, please.
(*Exit Denman.*)

VIOLET: Charles, if you are determined upon this investigation
Which I am convinced is going to lead us nowhere,
And which I am sure Amy would disapprove of—

I only wish to express my emphatic protest
Both against your purpose and the means you are employing.
    CHARLES: My purpose is, to find out what's wrong with Harry:
Until we know that, we can do nothing for him.
And as for my means, we can't afford to be squeamish
In taking hold of anything that comes to hand.
If you are interested in helping Harry
You can hardly object to the means.
    VIOLET: I do object.
    IVY: And I wish to associate myself with my sister
In her objections—
    AGATHA: I have no objection,
Any more than I object to asking Dr. Warburton:
I only see that this is all quite irrelevant;
We had better leave Charles to talk to Downing
And pursue his own methods.
    (*Rises.*)
    VIOLET: I do not agree.
I think there should be witnesses. I intend to remain.
And I wish to be present to hear what Downing says.
I want to know at once, not be told about it later.
    IVY: And I shall stay with Violet.
    AGATHA: I shall return
When Downing has left you.
    (*Exit.*)
    CHARLES: Well, I'm very sorry
You all see it like this: but there simply are times
When there's nothing to do but take the bull by the horns,
And this is one.
    (*Knock: and enter Downing.*)
                Good evening, Downing.
It's good to see you again, after all these years.
You're well, I hope?
    DOWNING: Thank you, very well indeed, Sir.
    CHARLES: I'm sorry to send for you so abruptly,
But I've a question I'd like to put to you,
I'm sure you won't mind, it's about his Lordship.
You've looked after his Lordship for over ten years . . .
    DOWNING: Eleven years, Sir, next Lady Day.
    CHARLES: Eleven years, and you know him pretty well.

And I'm sure that you've been a good friend to him, too.
We haven't seen him for nearly eight years,
And to tell the truth, now that we've seen him,
We're a little worried about his health.
He doesn't seem to be . . . quite himself.
    DOWNING: Quite natural, if I may say so, Sir,
After what happened.
    CHARLES: Quite so, quite.
Downing, you were with them on the voyage from New York—
We didn't learn very much about the circumstances;
We only knew what we read in the papers—
Of course, there was a great deal too much in the papers.
Downing, do you think that it might have been suicide,
And that his Lordship knew it?
    DOWNING: Unlikely, Sir, if I may say so.
Much more likely to have been an accident.
I mean, knowing her Ladyship
I don't think she had the courage.
    CHARLES: Did she ever talk of suicide?
    DOWNING: Oh yes, she did, every now and again
But in my opinion, it is those that talk
That are the least likely. To my way of thinking
She only did it to frighten people.
If you take my meaning—just for the effect.
    CHARLES: I understand, Downing. Was she in good spirits?
    DOWNING: Well, always about the same, Sir.
What I mean is, always up and down.
Down in the morning, and up in the evening,
And *then* she used to get rather excited,
And, in a way, irresponsible, Sir,
If I may make so bold, Sir,
I always thought that a very few cocktails
Went a long way with her Ladyship.
She wasn't one of those that are *designed* for drinking;
It's natural for some and unnatural for others.
    CHARLES: And how was his Lordship, during the voyage?
    DOWNING: Well, you might say depressed, Sir.
But you know his Lordship was always very quiet:
Very uncommon that I saw him in high spirits.
For what my judgement's worth, I always said his Lordship

Suffered from what they call a kind of repression.
But what struck me . . . more nervous than usual;
I mean to say, you could see that he was nervous.
He behaved as if he thought something might happen.
>CHARLES: What sort of thing?
>DOWNING: Well, I don't know, Sir.
But he seemed very anxious about my Lady.
Tried to keep near her when the weather was rough,
Didn't like to see her lean over the rail.
He was in a rare fright, once or twice.
But you know, it is just my opinion, Sir,
That his Lordship is rather psychic, as they say.
>CHARLES: Were they always together?
>DOWNING: Always, Sir.
That was just my complaint against my Lady.
It's my opinion that man and wife
Shouldn't see too much of each other, Sir.
Quite the contrary of the usual opinion,
I dare say. She wouldn't leave him alone.
And there's my complaint against these ocean liners
With all their swimming baths and gymnasiums
There's not even a place where a man can go
For a quiet smoke, where the woman can't follow him.
She wouldn't leave him out of her sight.
>CHARLES: During that evening, did you see him?
>DOWNING: Oh yes, Sir, I'm sure I saw him.
I don't mean to say that he had any orders—
His Lordship is always most considerate
About keeping me up. But when I say I saw him,
I mean that I saw him accidental.
You see, Sir, I was down in the Tourist,
And I took a bit of air before I went to bed,
And you could see the corner of the upper deck.
And I remember, there I saw his Lordship
Leaning over the rail, looking at the water—
There wasn't a moon, but I was sure it was him.
While I took my turn about, for nearly half an hour
He stayed there alone, looking over the rail.
Her Ladyship must have been all right then,
Mustn't she, Sir? or else he'd have known it.

CHARLES: Oh yes . . . quite so. Thank you, Downing,
I don't think we need you any more.
    GERALD: Oh, Downing,
Is there anything wrong with his Lordship's car?
    DOWNING: Oh no, Sir, she's in good running order:
I see to that.
    GERALD: I only wondered
Why you've been busy about it tonight.
    DOWNING: Nothing wrong, Sir:
Only I like to have her always ready.
Would there be anything more, Sir?
    GERALD: Thank you, Downing;
Nothing more.
    (*Exit Downing.*)
    VIOLET: Well, Charles, I must say, with your investigations,
You seem to have left matters much as they were—
Except for having brought Downing into it:
Of which I disapprove.
    CHARLES: Of which you disapprove.
But I believe that an unconscious accomplice is desirable.
    CHORUS: Why should we stand here like guilty conspirators,
    waiting for some revelation
When the hidden shall be exposed, and the newsboy shall shout
    in the street?
When the private shall be made public, the common photographer
Flashlight for the picture papers: why do we huddle together
In a horrid amity of misfortune? why should we be implicated,
brought in and brought together?
    IVY: I do not trust Charles with his confident vulgarity,
acquired from worldly associates.
    GERALD: Ivy is only concerned for herself, and her credit
among her shabby genteel acquaintance.
    VIOLET: Gerald is certain to make some blunder, he is useless
out of the army.
    CHARLES: Violet is afraid that her status as Amy's sister will
be diminished.
    CHORUS: We all of us make the pretension
To be the uncommon exception
To the universal bondage.
We like to appear in the newspapers

So long as we are in the right column.
We know about the railway accident
We know about the sudden thrombosis
And the slowly hardening artery.
We like to be thought well of by others
So that we may think well of ourselves.
And any explanation will satisfy:
We only ask to be reassured
About the noises in the cellar
And the window that should not have been open.
Why do we all behave as if the door might suddenly open, the
     curtains be drawn,
The cellar make some dreadful disclosure, the roof disappear,
And we should cease to be sure of what is real or unreal?
Hold tight, hold tight, we must insist that the world is what we
     have always taken it to be.
     AMY'S VOICE: Ivy! Violet! has Arthur or John come yet?
     IVY: There is no news of Arthur or John.
     (*Enter Amy and Agatha.*)
     AMY: It is very annoying. They both promised to be here
In good time for dinner. It is very annoying.
Now they can hardly arrive in time to dress.
I do not understand what could have gone wrong
With both of them, coming from different directions.
Well, we must go and dress, I suppose. I hope Harry will feel better
After his rest upstairs.
     (*Exeunt.*)

THE FIRSTBORN

(Act I, Scene I)

by

Christopher Fry

CHARACTERS

ANATH BITHIAH, *Pharaoh's sister.*
TEUSRET, *Pharaoh's daughter.*
SETI THE SECOND, *the Pharaoh.*
RAMASES, *his son.*
MOSES.
AARON, *his brother.*
A GUARD.

THE AUTHOR

Christopher Fry was born in England in 1907, and is what may be called 'a man of the theatre'. He has worked as an actor and producer, as well as a playwright, for most of his life, and this has given him a remarkable grasp of the technical requirements of the stage. He began writing plays in the thirties, but it was not until after 1945 that he became recognized as a brilliant new talent. His major plays have been *A Phoenix Too Frequent, The Lady's Not For Burning* (which had a remarkable commercial success), *Venus Observed*, and *A Sleep of Prisoners. The Firstborn* was begun in 1938 but was not completed until 1945. It was first presented at the Edinburgh Festival in 1948.

In recent years, Fry has concentrated on translating and adapting the works of the two important French playwrights, Jean Anouilh and Jean Giraudoux.

THE PLAY

The Firstborn is based on the story of the captivity of the Jews by the Pharaoh of Egypt and their escape under the leadership of Moses. Moses has been brought up as a prince of Egypt, having been adopted by the present Pharaoh's sister, but has become aware of himself as a Jew and has left the country. He intercedes with God on behalf of the Israelites and returns to Egypt—this is the point where the play begins. Moses then learns the agonizing truth that the freedom of the Israelites may only be obtained at the cost of the death of the firstborn of every family in Egypt. This means that Pharaoh's son, Ramases, must die, and he is a boy with great humanity for whom Moses has considerable affection. But the sacrifice must be made; Moses learns that man seldom has a simple choice—freedom may be obtained but only at a price, in this case Ramases' death.

It is worth noting here that, in most of his plays, Fry has used periods of remote time as his settings. In this way, he avoids Eliot's dilemma—how to make poetic speech acceptable in a play set in our own time.

THE FIRSTBORN

Act I, Scene I

*The scene is the terrace of the palace of Seti the Second, Pharaoh
of Egypt, at Tanis. A morning in the summer of* 1200 B.C. *A flight
of steps (unseen) leads down through a gate to open ground. The
terrace looks out upon an incompleted pyramid.*

A scream.

*Enter from the palace Anath Bithiah, a woman of fifty, sister to the
Pharaoh, and Teusret, a girl of fifteen, the Pharaoh's daughter.*

ANATH: What was it, Teusret?

TEUSRET: Did you hear it too?

ANATH: Some man is dead. That scream was password to a
grave.
Look there: up go the birds!

TEUSRET: The heat on this terrace!
You could bake on these stones, Aunt Anath.

ANATH: Ask who it was.

TEUSRET: They're working steadily at father's tomb.
There's no sign of trouble.

ANATH: We're too far off to see.
We should know more if we could see their faces.

TEUSRET: *(calling down the steps)* Guard! Come up here.

ANATH: I should like to be certain.
Oh, that pyramid! Everyday, watching it build,
Will make an old woman of me early.
It will cast a pretty shadow when it's done.
Two hundred more men were taken on today.
Did you know that Teusret? Your father's in a hurry.
Their sweat would be invaluable to the farmers in this drought.
What pains they take to house a family of dust.

TEUSRET: It's a lovely tomb.

ANATH: Yes, so it may be.
But what shall we do with all that air to breathe
And no more breath? I could as happily lie
And wait for eternal life in something smaller.

(*Enter a guard.*)

TEUSRET: What was that scream we heard?

GUARD: It's nothing, madam.

ANATH: You are right. Nothing. It was something once
But now it is only a scare of birds in the air
And a pair of women with their nerves uncovered;
Nothing.

TEUSRET: Who was it screamed?

GUARD: One of the builders
Missed his footing, madam; merely an Israelite.
They're digging him into the sand. No, over to the left.

TEUSRET: Oh yes, I see them now.—That was all I wanted.

(*Exit the guard.*)
So that's all right.

ANATH: Can you remember your cousin?

TEUSRET: Why, which cousin?

ANATH: My foster son. You knew him
When you were little. He lived with us in the palace.

TEUSRET: The birds are back on the roof now.

ANATH: Moses, Teusret.

TEUSRET: What, Aunt? Yes, I think I remember. I remember
A tall uncle. Was he only a cousin?
He used to drum his helmet with his dagger
While he sang us regimental marches to get us to sleep.
It never did. Why?

ANATH: No reason. I thought of him.
Well, they've buried the man in the sand. We'd better
Find our morning again and use what's left.

TEUSRET: Why did you think of him? Why *then* particularly?

ANATH: Why not then? Sometimes he blows about my brain
Like litter at the end of a public holiday.
I have obstinate affections. Ask your father.
He would tell you, if it wasn't impolitic
To mention Moses, what a girl of fire
I was, before I made these embers.
He could tell you how I crossed your grandfather,
And your grandfather was a dynasty in himself.
Oh Teusret, what a day of legend that was!
I held forbidden Israel in my arms
And growled on my stubborn doorstep, till I had my way.

TEUSRET: What do you mean?

ANATH: Well never mind.

TEUSRET: I do.
You've told me so far.

ANATH: Keep it to yourself then.
The summer of '24 had brilliant days
And unprecedented storms. The striped linen
You once cut up for a doll's dress was the dress
Made for me that summer. It was the summer
When my father, your grandfather, published the pronouncement.

TEUSRET: What pronouncement?

ANATH: That all the boys of Jewdom
Should be killed. Not out of spite, Teusret; necessity.
Your grandfather ordered that Defence of the Realm be painted
At the head of the document, in azure and silver.
It made it easier for him.

TEUSRET: Were they killed?

ANATH: Yes, they all died of a signature. Or we thought so,
Until the thirtieth of August. I went bathing on that day.
I was a girl then, Teusret, and played with the Nile
As though with a sister. And afterwards as I waded
To land again, pushing the river with my knees,
The wash rocked a little ark out
Into the daylight: and in the ark I found
A tiny weeping Israel who had failed
To be exterminated. When I stooped
With my hair dripping on to his face
He stopped in a screwed-up wail and looked.
And when I found my hands and crowded him
Into my breast, he buried like a burr.
And when I spoke I laughed, and when I laughed
I cried, he was so enchanting. I was ready
To raise a hornet's nest to keep him; in fact
I raised one. All the court flew up and buzzed.
But what could they do? Not even my Pharaoh-father
Could sting him out of my arms. So he grew up
Into your tall cousin, Egyptian
From beard to boots and, what was almost better,
A soldier of genius. You don't remember

How I held you on this terrace, to see him come home from war?
It was ten years ago. Do you remember
The shrieking music, and half Egypt shouting
Conqueror! Peacemaker!

TEUSRET: No.

ANATH: They have all tried to forget.
They have blotted him out of the records, but not out
Of my memory.

TEUSRET: Why did they blot him out?

ANATH: I might have known that I should say too much.

TEUSRET: Aunt, you must tell me.

ANATH: Well, no doubt I meant to.
The day I held you here, he came as the conqueror
Of Abyssinia. In all the windows and doors
Women elbowed and cracked their voices; and men
Hung on the gates and trees; and children sang
The usual songs, conducted by their teachers.

TEUSRET: Yes, but what happened to make him—

ANATH: All right, I'm coming to it, Teusret. The day after,
For the country-side also to be able to see their hero,
He went to inspect the city being built at Pithom.—
My book was closed from that day forward.
He went round with an officer who unfortunately
Was zealous but unintelligent. Silly man:
Silly, silly man. He found a labourer
Idling or resting, and he thought, I suppose,
'I'll show this prince that I'm worth my position'
And beat the workman. A Jewish bricklayer.
He beat him senseless.

TEUSRET: And then?

ANATH: Moses turned—turned to what was going on—
Turned himself and his world turtle. It was
As though an inward knife scraped his eyes clean.
The General of Egypt, the Lion and the Prince
Recognized his mother's face in the battered body
Of a bricklayer; saw it was not the face above
His nursery, not my face after all.
He knew his seed. And where my voice had hung till then
Now voices descending from ancestral Abraham
Congregated on him. And he killed

His Egyptian self in the self of that Egyptian
And buried that self in the sand.

TEUSRET: Aunt—
(*Enter a guard.*)

GUARD: The Pharaoh.
Madam, the Pharaoh is here.

ANATH: Can we look innocent?
(*Enter Seti. Exit the guard.*)

TEUSRET: Good morning, father.

SETI: Go indoors, my Teusret.
(*Exit Teusret.*)
Where is Moses?

ANATH: Seti!

SETI: Where is Moses? You will know.
In what country? Doing what?

ANATH: Why Moses?

SETI: I need him.

ANATH: I've no reason to remember.
I'm without him.

SETI: But you know.

ANATH: Why should I know?
Why should I? When the sun goes down do I have to know
Where and how it grovels under the world?
I thought he was a dust-storm we had shut outside.
Even now I sometimes bite on the grit.

SETI: I have found him necessary.
Libya is armed along the length of her frontier,
And the South's like sand, shifting and uncertain.
I need Moses.—We have discarded in him
A general of excellent perception.

ANATH: He's discarded, rightly or wrongly. We've let him go.

SETI: Deeds lie down at last, and so did his.
Out in the wilderness, after two days' flight,
His deed lay down, knowing what it had lost him.
Under the boredom of thorn-trees his deed cried out
For Egypt and died. Ten years long he has lugged
This dead thing after him. His loyalty needn't be questioned.

ANATH: We're coming to something strange when a normal day
Opens and lets in the past. He may remember
Egypt. He's in Midian.

SETI: In what part of Midian?

ANATH: Wherever buckets are fetched up out of wells
Or in his grave.

SETI: We'll find him. If we have to comb
Midian to its shadows we'll find him.

ANATH: He's better where he is.

SETI: He is essential to my plans.

ANATH: I tell you
He is better where he is. For you or me
He's better where he is.
We have seen different days without him
And I have done my hair a different way.
Leave him alone to bite his lips.
    (*Seti's eye is caught by something below and beyond the terrace.*)

SETI: What's this,
What is this crowd?

ANATH: It's Ramases! No qualms
For the dynasty, with a son as popular as he is.

SETI: There's half the city round him. Where are his guards?

ANATH: There: a little behind.

SETI: The boy's too careless.
I'm not altogether at rest in the way he's growing,
His good graces for no-matter-whom.
He must learn to let the needs of Egypt rule him.

ANATH: He will learn. He is learning.

SETI: Egypt should pray so.

ANATH: I would hazard a guess that Egypt's women
Have prayed for him often enough. Ra, rising
An eyebrow stiff with the concentration of creation
Probably says: That boy again? We'd better
Make something of him early and have them satisfied.
O, Ramases will be all right.

SETI: I hope,
I hope.
    (*Enter Ramases, a boy of eighteen.*)

RAMASES: Did you see the excitement? I think it's the drought.
Like the air, we're all quivering with heat.
Do you find that, Aunt? Either you must sleep like the dead
Or something violent must happen.

ANATH: Look: your father.

RAMASES: I didn't see you, father. I'm sorry, sir.
Did I interrupt state matters?

SETI: What morning have you had?

RAMASES: Holiday—books rolled up, military exercises
Over, and no social engagements. I've been fowling
Down at the marshes.

ANATH: Any luck?

RAMASES: Not much flesh
But a paradise of feathers. I was out before daybreak.

ANATH: It's a good marksman who hunts by batlight.

RAMASES: But I
Waited for daylight. Until then the marsh was a torpor.
I clucked and clapped as the sun rose
And up shot so much whistle and whirr
I could only hold my spear and laugh.
All the indignant wings of the marshes
Flocking to the banner of Tuesday
To avoid the Prince of Egypt!
Off they flapped into the mist
Looking about for Monday
The day they had lived in peace: and finding nothing
Back they wheeled to Tuesday.
I had recovered myself by then and killed
One that had the breast of a chestnut.
At last he could feel the uninterrupted darkness
Of an addled egg. I watched his nerves flinching
As they felt how dark that darkness was.
I found myself trying to peer into his death.
It seemed a long way down. The morning and it
Were oddly separate,
Though the bird lay in the sun: separate somehow
Even from contemplation.

ANATH: Excellent spirits
To make a success of a holiday.

RAMASES: Only for a moment.

SETI: This afternoon I have business for you.
(He turns to go in.)

RAMASES: Very well.

SETI: Was that thunder?

ANATH: They're dumping new stone for the pyramid.

RAMASES: Two men came through the marshes before I left;
Jews, but not our Jews: or one of them
Was not; he seemed a man of prosperity
Although some miles of sun and dust were on him.
  SETI: Aliens?
  RAMASES: Yes; but one of them I felt
I should have known. How could I?
I passed them again as I came home. They stood
To watch the crowd. I looked across and smiled
But got no smiles from them. And one, the tall one—
  ANATH: Very tall?
  RAMASES: Yes, he was tall. It was he
Who is somehow in my memory.
  ANATH: Seti—
  SETI: Well?
  ANATH: Is it possible that someone hasn't waited to be recalled?
Is it possible?
  SETI: It is not possible.
  ANATH: Your thoughts are leaning that way too.
Sometimes the unaccountable stalks in.
  SETI: Which way were they travelling, Ramases?
  RAMASES: This way. If I had only thought of them sooner
We could have seen them go by.—Sir!
They are standing here at the foot of the stairway. How long
Can they have been there? Shall I speak to them?
  ANATH: He has stood all day under my brain's stairway.
Seti, who is there? Which foremost, Ramases?
The tall one?
  RAMASES: Yes. Who's in your mind?
  ANATH: The tall one.
The tall one.
  (*Ramases goes down the steps.*)
                              So he is back; and small-talk
Has to block a draught up ten years old.
  SETI: Why has he come?
  ANATH: You said he longed for Egypt.
  SETI: I think so.
  ANATH: But what am I in Egypt?
A dead king's daughter.
  (*Re-enter Ramases followed by Moses and Aaron.*)

SETI: What words can I find to fit
So ghostly a homecoming? Understand you are welcome.
Whatever uncertainty you have can go.
We welcome you. Look who is here.

ANATH: He has seen me. We have looked at one another.

SETI: We'll absolve ourselves of the ten years. Who is this?

MOSES: My brother.

SETI: I had not heard you had a brother.

ANATH: A brother, a sister—and a mother. All the three.

SETI: I told my sister we must have you back.
And so we must, and so Egypt must; and it seems
That we have. You are come promptly at the word, Moses.

MOSES: This is not why I came.

SETI: You would scarcely forsee it.

MOSES: I am not who you think. I am a stranger.

SETI: Not by a vein or a hair. The past is forgotten.
You are a prince of Egypt.

MOSES: The prince of Egypt
Died the day he fled.

SETI: What do you mean?

MOSES: That prince of Egypt died. I am the Hebrew
Smitten out of the shadow of that prince,
Vomited out of his dry lips, the cry
Whipped off the sanded tongue of that prince of Egypt.

SETI: What has this long discomfort done for you,
My friend? It has made you bitter.

MOSES: Make no mistake;
I have done very well for myself. I haven't come to beg.
Why was it you decided to ask me to come back?

SETI: Isn't it time we laid the crippling ghost
That haunts us? You evidently thought so too
To come so far.

MOSES: You've a better reason than that.

SETI: Why should you want reasons when you have come
On your own initiative? Why are you here?
I am asking you candidly. Why did you come?

MOSES: My blood heard my blood weeping
Far off like the swimming of fear under the sea,
The sobbirg at night below the garden. I heard
My blood weeping. It is here it wept and weeps.

It was from here I heard coming this drum of despair,
Under your shoes, under your smile, and under
The foundations of your tomb. From Egypt.
    ANATH: What was it, Seti, that lay down and died?
    SETI: Why are you here?
    MOSES: To be close to this
That up to now has only made me uneasy,
As though a threat of evil whispered beyond
Control under the wind. I could be
Uneasy and still eat in Midian.
I could be Pharaoh in Midian, but in Egypt
I knew I should be Moses.
    SETI: Still you haven't
Answered my question. Come, what do you want?
    MOSES: First, that you should know what you are doing.
    SETI: Take care, Moses.
    ANATH: And secondly?
    MOSES: What can I hope
From that until he has understood the first?
    SETI: What is this mood you have come in which is so ready
To abuse a decent welcome? There is something shipwreck
About you that will not do for peaceful places.
Steady yourself if we're to understand one another.
I am the Pharaoh, Moses, not the young uncle
Of the Heliopolis classroom, not your messroom brother.
    MOSES: A man has more to be than a Pharaoh.
He must dare to outgrow the security
Of partial blindness. I am not speaking now
To your crown; I'm speaking to your merciless mischief.
    SETI: You have coarsened during your exile. What you say
Hasn't even the virtue of clarity. If you wish
To consider my offer of reinstatement, go
And consider. I can be patient. Egypt can do
Her work on you like a generous woman, given
Her time.
    (*He glances at Anath.*)
            Midian will wash off in the Nile.
Go on, go on, I shall not remember this morning.
    MOSES: I think you will. My brother has lived these days
In amongst Israel, while I was sleeping.

He knows both the truth and the injury better than I can.
Let him speak what he knows.

    AARON: Twelve hundred thousand Israelites are under
Your dominion. Of these two hundred and twenty thousand
Only, are men. The rest are in the proportion
Of four hundred and fifty thousand women
And five hundred and thirty thousand children.

    SETI: I have my census-takers.

    AARON: So perhaps
Has Death got his; but I think he has not referred
His undertakings to your dynastic understanding.
Here I have his estimate: between April and July
Six hundred and one deaths suffered in old age
But an old age of forced labour, their backs bent twice,
Under the weight of years and under the mule-whip.
Also thirty-eight deaths of healthy men
Who made some show of reluctance or momentary
Impatience.

    MOSES: That was a good cure. They are now
Patient for all eternity.

    AARON: Also the deaths
Of a hundred pregnant women, forced to dig
Until they had become their own gravediggers.
Also the deaths of eighty-four children, twelve
Unofficial crucifixions . . .

    SETI: This is intolerable
Singsong! Am I to compose the epitaphs
For every individual grave of this trying summer?
I have my figures. I do not need yours.
I have put men to a purpose who otherwise
Would have had not the least meaning.

    MOSES: Not the least meaning, except the meaning
Of the breath in your lungs, the mystery of existing
At all. What have we approached or conceived
When we have conquered and built a world? Even
Though civilization became perfect? What then?
We have only put a crown on the skeleton.
It is the individual man
In his individual freedom who can mature
With his warm spirit the unripe world.

They are your likeness, these men, even to nightmares.
I have business with Egypt, one more victory for her,
A better one than Ethiopia:
That she should come to see her own shame
And discover justice for my people.

SETI: You have fermented in your Midian bottle.
But lately I have learnt an obstinate patience.
We should have done better to have met
Out of the sun. We can do better than this
And so we shall yet, later, at a cooler time.
Where will you sleep? We will see you have food.
Do you remember, I wonder, the palace nectarine?
I said, where will you lodge?

MOSES:　　　　　　　　　With my sister, Miriam.

SETI: (*to Anath*) Do you know where that is?

ANATH:　　　　　　　　　　Perfectly.

SETI: (*going in*)　　　　　　　Very well.

ANATH: Now he will not sleep again tonight.

MOSES: I hope that none of us will sleep again
Until we all can sleep.

ANATH:　　　　　　　And so once more
We see each other. You have chosen a fine day.

(*Moses waits. Anath says no more. He goes with Aaron.*)

ANATH: I taught him to walk, Ramases. I also taught him
To speak and say his alphabet. I taught you your
Alphabet also; and also Teusret hers.
I have been a really useful woman.

RAMASES:　　　　　　　　　Where
Does his sister live?

ANATH:　　　　　　　Why do you want to know?

RAMASES: I wondered where it might be.

ANATH:　　　　　　　　　　She has a tent
By the brick-kiln.

RAMASES: I liked that man.

ANATH: So have others before you. Like him, Ramases,
Forget him, and let us live in peace.

RAMASES: I shall go and find him.

ANATH: Ramases, I ask you to forget him.

RAMASES:　　　　　　　　　How?

ANATH: What would make it difficult?

RAMASES: Can you forget him?
ANATH: He has gone.
RAMASES: And something of us, I think, went with him.
ANATH: Well, you will let him go. I have asked you.
RAMASES: No.
I love you, you know that. But trust me a little.
I shall be discreet.
　　(*Exit Ramases.*)
ANATH: Ramases! —No,
What should I be doing, turning his feet
Towards my fears?
　　(*She goes to the parapet. Enter Teusret.*)
TEUSRET: Aunt Anath—
ANATH: Do you remember, Teusret?
A man fell from the pyramid—only this morning.

Plays from Ireland and America

JUNO AND THE PAYCOCK

(Act I)

by

Sean O'Casey

CHARACTERS

'CAPTAIN' JACK BOYLE.
JUNO BOYLE, *his wife*
JOHNNY BOYLE ⎱ *their children.*
MARY BOYLE ⎰
'JOXER' DALY.
JERRY DEVINE.
A COAL VENDOR.
CHARLIE BENTHAM, *a school teacher.*
A BEARDED MAN.

THE AUTHOR

Sean O'Casey was born in 1884 in the slums of Dublin, about which he writes so vividly, and died in England in 1964. He was largely self-educated, and worked as a dock-worker, builder's labourer and stone-breaker on the roads before he established a reputation as one of the most important playwrights of the twentieth century. In his youth he was an Irish patriot and was involved in the struggle for Ireland's independence, but he quarrelled with the famous Irish theatre, the Abbey, in 1926 and thereafter lived in England. His first play to be produced was *Shadow of a Gunman*, in 1923. This was followed by *Juno and the Paycock* and *The Plough and the Stars*, these three plays being his best known. His plays are a strange mixture of comedy (in fact, near farce) and tragedy. For this, he has been criticized by some and praised by others. His critics say one does not know whether to laugh at his character's misfortunes or cry; his supporters say that O'Casey shows us, better than anyone else, how farce and tragedy seem to be mingled in human affairs.

THE PLAY

Juno and the Paycock is a picture of a down-and-out Dublin family kept together by a sharp-tongued and courageous wife, the Juno of the title. Her husband, 'Captain' Jack Boyle, idles his time away, boasting of his imaginary adventures, with his drinking companion, Joxer Daly. Her daughter, Mary, is interested in the labour movement and is on strike. Her son, Johnny, has lost an arm and been wounded in the Irish Rebellion, but has betrayed a comrade and lives in fear of his life. Only Juno is working; without her the family would go to pieces. Unexpectedly, the Boyles have a stroke of luck. They are left some money and proceed to refurnish their home on credit. But then tragedy strikes. Mary is deserted by her new suitor, Charlie Bentham, a schoolteacher; Johnny is taken away and executed by the I.R.A.; and it turns out that the legacy is non-existent. In the end, Juno is in a worse plight than before, and her tragedy is heightened by the return of her husband and Joxer, roaring drunk, singing patriotic Irish songs.

O'Casey has never been popular in Ireland, mainly because of his shrewd assessment of the Irish character. Responding to sudden enthusiasms and violent action, it is, he seems to think,

essentially unstable. In this play, only Juno seems to have a sense of responsibility; the others live in a half-world of vague longings and imaginary grandeur. O'Casey's method of writing plays is not only to point out the farcical nature of such a situation, but to show that within it lie the seeds of deplorable tragedy. If this is accepted, then his plays must be considered brilliantly successful.

JUNO AND THE PAYCOCK

Act I

The living room of a two-room tenancy occupied by the Boyle family in a tenement house in Dublin. Left, a door leading to another part of the house; left of door a window looking into the street; at back a dresser; farther to the right at back, a window looking into the back of the house. Between the window and the dresser is a picture of the Virgin; below the picture, on a bracket, is a crimson bowl in which a floating votive light is burning. Farther to the right is a small bed partly concealed by cretonne hangings strung on a twine. To the right is the fireplace; near the fireplace is a door leading to the other room. Beside the fireplace is a box containing coal. On the mantelpiece is an alarm clock lying on its face. In a corner near the window looking into the back is a galvanized bath. A table and some chairs. On the table are breakfast things for one. A teapot is on the hob and a frying pan stands inside the fender. There are a few books on the dresser and one on the table. Leaning against the dresser is a long-handled shovel— the kind invariably used by labourers when turning concrete or mixing mortar. Johnny Boyle is sitting crouched beside the fire. Mary with her jumper off—it is lying on the back of a chair—is arranging her hair before a tiny mirror perched on the table. Beside the mirror is stretched out the morning paper, which she looks at when she isn't gazing into the mirror. She is a well-made and good-looking girl of twenty-two. Two forces are working in her mind—one, through the circumstances of her life, pulling her back; the other, through the influence of books she has read, pushing her forward. The opposing forces are apparent in her speech and her manners, both of which are degraded by her environment, and improved by her acquaintance—slight though it be— with literature. The time is early forenoon.

MARY: (*looking at the paper*) On a little bye-road, out beyant Finglas, he was found.

(*Mrs. Boyle enters by door on right; she has been shopping and carries a small parcel in her hand. She is forty-five years of age, and twenty years ago she must have been a pretty woman; but her face has now assumed that look which ultimately settles down upon the*

117

faces of the women of the working class; a look of listless monotony and harassed anxiety, blending with an expression of mechanical resistance. Were circumstances favourable, she would probably be a handsome, active and clever woman.)

MRS. BOYLE: Isn't he come in yet?

MARY: No, mother.

MRS. BOYLE: Oh, he'll come in when he likes; struttin' about the town like a paycock with Joxer, I suppose. I hear all about Mrs. Tancred's son is in this mornin's paper.

MARY: The full details are in it this mornin'; seven wounds he had—one entherin' the neck, with an exit wound beneath the left shoulder-blade; another in the left breast penethratin' the heart, an' . . .

JOHNNY: (*springing up from the fire*) Oh, quit that readin', for God's sake! Are yous losin' all your feelin's? It'll soon be that none of yous'll read anythin' that's not about butcherin'! (*He goes quickly into the room on left.*)

MARY: He's gettin' very sensitive, all of a sudden!

MRS. BOYLE: I'll read it myself, Mary, by an' by, when I come home. Everybody's sayin' that he was a die-hard—thanks be to God that Johnny had nothin' to do with him this long time . . . (*Opening the parcel and taking out some sausages, which she places on a plate.*) Ah, then, if that father o' yours doesn't come in soon for his breakfast, he may go without any; I'll not wait much longer for him.

MARY: Can't you let him get it himself when he comes in?

MRS. BOYLE: Yes, an' let him bring in Joxer Daly along with him? Ay, that's what he'd like, an' that's what he's waitin' for—till he thinks I'm gone to work, an' then sail in with the boul' Joxer, to burn all the coal an' dhrink all the tea in the place, to show them what a good Samaritan he is! But I'll stop here till he comes in, if I have to wait till tomorrow mornin'.

VOICE OF JOHNNY: (*inside*) Mother!

MRS. BOYLE: Yis?

VOICE OF JOHNNY: Bring us in a dhrink o' wather.

MRS. BOYLE: Bring in that fella a dhrink o' wather, for God's sake, Mary.

MARY: Isn't he big an' able enough to come out an' get it himself?

MRS. BOYLE: If you weren't well yourself you'd like somebody to bring you in a dhrink o' wather. (*She brings in drink and returns.*) Isn't it terrible to have to be waitin' this way! You'd think he was bringin' twenty poun's a week into the house the way he's goin' on. He wore out the Health Insurance long ago, he's afther wearin' out the unemployment dole, an', now, he's thryin' to wear out me! An' constantly singin', no less, when he ought always to be on his knees offerin' up a Novena for a job!

MARY: (*tying a ribbon, fillet-wise around her head*) I don't like this ribbon, ma; I think I'll wear the green—it looks betther than the blue.

MRS. BOYLE: Ah, wear whatever ribbon you like, girl, only don't be botherin' me. I don't know what a girl on strike wants to be wearin' a ribbon round her head for or silk stockin's on her legs either; it's wearin' them things that make the employers think they're givin' yous too much money.

MARY: The hour is past now when we'll ask the employers' permission to wear what we like.

MRS. BOYLE: I don't know why you wanted to walk out for Jennie Claffey; up to this you never had a good word for her.

MARY: What's the use of belongin' to a Trades Union if you won't stand up for your principles? Why did they sack her? It was a clear case of victimization. We couldn't let her walk the streets, could we?

MRS. BOYLE: No, of course yous couldn't—yous wanted to keep her company. Wan victim wasn't enough. When the employers sacrifice wan victim, the Trades Unions go wan betther be sacrificin' a hundred.

MARY: It doesn't matther what you say, ma—a principle's a principle.

MRS. BOYLE: Yis; an' when I go into oul' Murphy's tomorrow, an' he gets to know that, instead o' payin' all, I'm goin' to borry more, what'll he say when I tell him a principle's a principle? What'll we do if he refuses to give us any more on tick?

MARY: He daren't refuse—if he does, can't you tell him he's paid?

MRS. BOYLE: It's lookin' as if he was paid, whether he refuses or no.

(*Johnny appears at the door on left. He can be plainly seen now; he is a thin, delicate fellow, something younger than Mary. He has evidently gone through a rough time. His face is pale and drawn; there is a tremulous look of indefinite fear in his eyes. The left sleeve of his coat is empty, and he walks with a slight halt.*)

JOHNNY: I was lyin' down; I thought yous were gone. Oul' Simon Mackay is thrampin' about like a horse over me head, an' I can't sleep with him—they're like thunder-claps in me brain! The curse o'—God forgive me for goin' to curse!

MRS. BOYLE: There, now; go back and lie down again, an' I'll bring you in a nice cup o' tay.

JOHNNY: Tay, tay, tay! You're always thinkin' o' tay. If a man was dyin', you'd thry to make him swally a cup o' tay! (*He goes back.*)

MRS. BOYLE: I don't know what's goin' to be done with him. The bullet he got in the hip in Easter Week was bad enough, but the bomb that shattered his arm in the fight in O'Connell Street put the finishin' touch to him. I knew he was makin' a fool of himself. God knows I went down on me bended knees to him not to go agen the Free State.

MARY: He stuck to his principles, an', no matther how you may argue, ma, a principle's a principle.

VOICE OF JOHNNY: Is Mary goin' to stay here?

MARY: No, I'm not goin' to stay here; you can't expect me to be always at your beck an' call, can you?

VOICE OF JOHNNY: I won't stay here be meself!

MRS. BOYLE: Amn't I nicely handicapped with the whole o' yous! I don't know what any o' yous ud do without your ma. (*To Johnny*) Your father'll be here in a minute, an' if you want anythin', he'll get it for you.

JOHNNY: I hate assin' him for anythin' . . . He hates to be assed to stir . . . Is the light lightin' before the picture o' the Virgin?

MRS. BOYLE: Yis, yis! The wan inside to St. Anthony isn't enough, but he must have another wan to the Virgin here!

(*Jerry Devine enters hastily. He is about twenty-five, well-set, active and earnest. He is a type, becoming very common now in the Labour Movement, of a mind knowing enough to make the mass of his associates, who know less, a power, and too little to broaden that power for the benefit of all. Mary seizes her jumper and runs hastily into room left.*)

JERRY: (*breathlessly*) Where's the Captain, Mrs. Boyle; where's the Captain?

MRS. BOYLE: You may as well ass a body that: he's wherever Joxer Daly is—dhrinkin' in some snug or another.

JERRY: Father Farrell is just afther stoppin' me to tell me to run up an' get him to go to the new job that's goin' on in Rathmines; his cousin is foreman o' the job, an' Father Farrell was speakin' to him about poor Johnny an' his father bein' idle so long, an' the foreman told Father Farrell to send the Captain up an' he'd give him a start—I wonder where I'd find him?

MRS. BOYLE: You'll find he's ayther in Ryan's or Foley's.

JERRY: I'll run round to Ryan's—I know it's a great house o' Joxer's. (*He rushes out.*)

MRS. BOYLE: (*piteously*) There now, he'll miss that job, or I know for what! If he gets win' o' the word, he'll not come back till evenin', so that it'll be too late. There'll never be any good got out o' him so long as he goes with that shouldher-shruggin' Joxer. I killin' meself workin', and he sthruttin' about from mornin' till night like a paycock!

(*The steps of two people are heard coming up a flight of stairs. They are the footsteps of Captain Boyle and Joxer. Captain Boyle is singing in a deep, sonorous, self-honouring voice.*)

THE CAPTAIN: Sweet spirit, hear me prayer! Hear . . . oh . . . hear . . . me prayer . . . hear, oh, hear . . . Oh, he . . . ar . . . oh, he . . . ar . . . me . . . pray . . . er!

JOXER: (*outside*) Ah, that's a darlin' song, a daaarlin' song!

MRS. BOYLE: (*viciously*) Sweet spirit hear his prayer! Oh, then, I'll take me solemn affeydavey, it's not for a job he's prayin'!

(*She sits down on the bed so that the cretonne hangings hide her from the view of those entering. The Captain comes slowly in. He is a man of about sixty; stout, grey-haired and stocky. His neck is short, and his head looks like a stone ball that one sometimes sees on top of a gatepost. His cheeks, reddish-purple, are puffed out, as if he were always repressing an almost irrepressible ejaculation. On his upper lip is a crisp, tightly-cropped moustache; he carries himself with the upper part of his body slightly thrown back, and his stomach slightly thrust forward. His walk is a slow, consequential strut. His clothes are dingy, and he wears a faded seaman's cap with a glazed peak.*)

BOYLE: (*to Joxer, who is still outside*) Come on, come on in, Joxer; she's gone out long ago, man. If there's nothing else to be got, we'll furrage out a cup o' tay, anyway. It's the only bit I get in comfort when she's away. 'Tisn't Juno should be her pet name at all, but Deirdre of the Sorras, for she's always grousin'.

(*Joxer steps cautiously into the room. He may be younger than the Captain but he looks a lot older. His face is like a bundle of crinkled paper; his eyes have a cunning twinkle; he is spare and loosely built; he has a habit of constantly shrugging his shoulders with a peculiar twitching movement, meant to be ingratiating. His face is invariably ornamented with a grin.*)

JOXER: It's a terrible thing to be tied to a woman that's always grousin'. I don't know how you stick it—it ud put years on me. It's a good job she has to be so ofen away, for (*with a shrug*) when the cat's away, the mice can play!

BOYLE: (*with a commanding and complacent gesture*) Pull over to the fire, Joxer, an' we'll have a cup o' tay in a minute.

JOXER: Ah, a cup o' tay's a darlin' thing, a daaarlin' thing— the cup that cheers but doesn't . . .

(*Joxer's rhapsody is cut short by the sight of Juno coming forward and confronting the two cronies. Both are stupefied.*)

MRS. BOYLE: (*with sweet irony—poking the fire, and turning her head to glare at Joxer*) Pull over to the fire, Joxer Daly, an' we'll have a cup o' tay in a minute! Are you sure, now, you wouldn't like an egg?

JOXER: I can't stop, Mrs. Boyle; I'm in a desperate hurry, a desperate hurry.

MRS. BOYLE: Pull over to the fire, Joxer Daly; people is always far more comfortable here than they are in their own place.

(*Joxer makes hastily for the door. Boyle stirs to follow him; thinks of something to relieve the situation—stops and says suddenly*):

BOYLE: Joxer!

JOXER: (*at door, ready to bolt*) Yis?

BOYLE: You know the foreman o' that job that's goin' on down in Killesther, don't you, Joxer?

JOXER: (*puzzled*) Foreman—Killesther?

BOYLE: (*with a meaning look*) He's a butty o' yours, isn't he?

JOXER: (*the truth dawning on him*) The foreman at Killesther— oh, yis, yis. He's an oul' butty o' mine—oh, he's a darlin' man, a daarlin' man.

BOYLE: Oh, then, it's a sure thing. It's a pity we didn't go down at breakfast first thing this mornin'—we might ha' been working now; but you didn't know it then.

JOXER: (*with a shrug*) It's betther late than never.

BOYLE: It's nearly time we got a start, anyhow; I'm fed up knockin' round doin' nothin'. He promised you—gave you the straight tip?

JOXER: Yis. 'Come down on the blow o' dinner,' says he, 'an' I'll start you, an' any friend you like to brin' with you.' Ah, says I, you're a darlin' man, a daaarlin' man.

BOYLE: Well, it couldn't come at a betther time—we're a long time waitin' for it.

JOXER: Indeed we were; but it's a long lane that has no turnin'.

BOYLE: The blow up for dinner is at one—wait till I see what time it 'tis. (*He goes to the mantelpiece, and gingerly lifts the clock.*)

MRS. BOYLE: Min' now, how you go on fiddlin' with that clock—you know the least little thing sets it asthray.

BOYLE: The job couldn't come at a betther time; I'm feelin' in great fettle, Joxer. I'd hardly believe I ever had a pain in me legs, an' last week I was nearly crippled with them.

JOXER: That's betther and betther; ah, God never shut wan door but he opened another!

BOYLE: It's only eleven o'clock; we've lashins o' time. I'll slip into me oul' moleskins afther breakfast, an' we can saunther down at our ayse. (*Putting his hand on the shovel.*) I think, Joxer, we'd betther bring our shovels?

JOXER: Yis, Captain, yis; it's betther to go fully prepared an' ready for all eventualities. You bring your long-tailed shovel, an' I'll bring me navvy. We mighten' want them, an', then again, we might: for want of a nail the shoe was lost, for want of a shoe the horse was lost, an' for want of a horse the man was lost—aw, that's a darlin' proverb, a daarlin' . . .

(*As Joxer was finishing his sentence, Mrs. Boyle approaches the door and Joxer retreats hurriedly, She shuts the door with a bang.*)

BOYLE: (*suggestively*) We won't be long pullin' ourselves together agen when I'm workin' for a few weeks.

(*Mrs. Boyle takes no notice.*)

BOYLE: The foreman on the job is an oul' butty o' Joxer's; I have an idea that I know him meself. (*Silence.*) . . . There's a button off the back o' me moleskin trousers . . . If you leave out a needle and thread I'll sew it on meself . . . Thanks be to God, the pains in me legs is gone, anyhow!

MRS. BOYLE: (*with a burst*) Look here, Mr. Jacky Boyle, them yarns won't go down with Juno. I know you an' Joxer Daly of an oul' date, an', if you think you're able to come it over me with them fairy tales, you're in the wrong shop.

BOYLE: (*coughing subduedly to relieve the tenseness of the situation*) U-u-u-ugh.

MRS. BOYLE: Butty o' Joxer's! Oh, you'll do a lot o' good as long as you continue to be a butty o' Joxer's!

BOYLE: U-u-u-ugh.

MRS. BOYLE: Shovel! Ah, then, me boyo, you'd do far more work with a knife and fork than ever you'll do with a shovel! If there was e'er a genuine job goin' you'd be dh'other way about—not able to lift your arms with the pains in your legs! Your poor wife slavin' to keep the bit in your mouth, an' you gallivantin' about all day like a paycock!

BOYLE: It ud be betther for a man to be dead, betther for a man to be dead.

MRS. BOYLE: (*ignoring the interruption*) Everybody callin' you 'Captain', an' you only wanst on the wather, in an oul' collier from here to Liverpool, when anybody, to listen or look at you, ud take you for a second Christo For Columbus!

BOYLE: Are you never goin' to give us a rest?

MRS. BOYLE: Oh, you're never tired o' lookin' for a rest.

BOYLE: D'ye want to drive me out o' the house?

MRS. BOYLE: It ud be easier to dhrive you out o' the house than to dhrive you into a job. Here, sit down an' take your breakfast—it may be the last you'll get, for I don't know where the next is goin' to come from.

BOYLE: If I get this job we'll be all right.

MRS. BOYLE: Did ye see Jerry Devine?

BOYLE: (*testily*) No, I didn't see him.

MRS. BOYLE: No, but you seen Joxer. Well, he was here lookin' for you.

BOYLE: Well, let him look!

MRS. BOYLE: Oh, indeed, he may well look, for it ud be hard for him to see you, an' you stuck in Ryan's snug.

BOYLE: I wasn't in Ryan's snug—I don't go into Ryan's.

MRS. BOYLE: Oh, is there a mad dog there? Well, if you weren't in Ryan's you were in Foley's.

BOYLE: I'm tellin' you for the last three weeks I haven' tasted a dhrop of intoxicatin' liquor. I wasn't in ayther snug or dh'other—I could swear that on a prayer book—I'm as innocent as the child unborn!

MRS. BOYLE: Well, if you'd been in for your breakfast you'd ha' seen him.

BOYLE: (suspiciously) What does he want me for?

MRS. BOYLE: He'll be back any minute an' then you'll soon know.

BOYLE: I'll drop out an' see if I can meet him.

MRS. BOYLE: You'll sit down an' take your breakfast, an' let me go to me work, for I'm an hour late already waitin' for you.

BOYLE: You needn't ha' waited, for I'll take no breakfast—I've a little spirit left in me still!

MRS. BOYLE: Are you goin' to have your breakfast—yes or no?

BOYLE: (too proud to yield) I'll have no breakfast—yous can keep your breakfast. (Plaintively) I'll knock out a bit somewhere, never fear.

MRS. BOYLE: Nobody's goin' to coax you—don't think that. (She vigorously replaces the pan and the sausages in the press.)

BOYLE: I've a little spirit left in me still.

(Jerry Devine enters hastily.)

JERRY: Oh, here you are at last! I've been searchin' for you everywhere. The foreman in Foley's told me you hadn't left the snug with Joxer ten minutes before I went in.

MRS. BOYLE: An' he swearin' on the holy prayer book that he wasn't in no snug!

BOYLE: (to Jerry) What business is it o' yours whether I was in a snug or no? What do you want to be gallopin' about afther me for? Is a man not to be allowed to leave his house for a minute without havin' a pack o' spies, pimps and informers cantherin' at his heels?

JERRY: Oh, you're takin' a wrong view of it, Mr. Boyle; I was simply anxious to do you a good turn. I have a message for you from Father Farrell: he says that if you go to the job that's on in Rathmines, an' ask for Foreman Mangan, you'll get a start.

BOYLE: That's all right, but I don' want the motions of me body to be watched the way the asthronomer ud watch a star. If you're folleyin' Mary aself, you've no pereeogative to be folleyin' me. (*Suddenly catching his thigh.*) U-ugh, I'm afther gettin' a terrible twinge in me right leg!

MRS. BOYLE: Oh, it won't be very long now till it travels into his left wan. It's miraculous that whenever he scents a job in front of him, his legs begin to fail him! Then, me bucko, if you lose this chance, you may go an' furrage for yourself!

JERRY: This job'll last some time, too, Captain, an' as soon as the foundations are in, it'll be cushy enough.

BOYLE: Won't it be a climbin' job? How d'ye expect me to be able to go up a ladder with these legs? An', if I get up aself, how am I goin' to get down agen?

MRS. BOYLE: (*viciously*) Get wan o' the labourers to carry you down in a hod! You can't climb a laddher, but you can skip like a goat into a snug!

JERRY: I wouldn't let meself be let down that easy, Mr. Boyle; a little exercise, now, might do you all the good in the world.

BOYLE: It's a docther you should have been, Devine—maybe you know more about the pains in me legs than meself that has them?

JERRY: (*irritated*) Oh, I know nothin' about the pains in your legs; I've brought the message Father Farrell gave me, an' that's all I can do.

MRS. BOYLE: Here, sit down an' take your breakfast, an' go an' get ready; an' don't be actin' as if you couldn't pull a wing out of a dead bee.

BOYLE: I want no breakfast, I tell you; it ud choke me afther all that's been said. I've a little spirit left in me still.

MRS. BOYLE: Well, let's see your spirit then, an' go in at wanst an' put on your moleskin trousers!

BOYLE: (*moving towards the door left*) It ud be betther for a man to be dead! U-ugh! There's another twinge in me other leg! Nobody but meself knows the sufferin' I'm goin' through with the pains in these legs o' mine. (*He goes into the room on left as Mary comes out with her hat in her hand.*)

MRS. BOYLE: I'll have to push off now, for I'm terrible late already, but I was determined to stay an' hunt that Joxer this time. (*She goes off.*)

JERRY: Are you going out, Mary?

MARY: It looks like it when I'm putting on my hat, doesn't it?

JERRY: The bitther word agen, Mary.

MARY: You won't allow me to be friendly with you; if I thry, you deliberately misunderstand it.

JERRY: I didn't always misundherstand it; you were ofen delighted to have the arms of Jerry around you.

MARY: If you go on talkin' like this, Jerry Devine, you'll make me hate you!

JERRY: Well, let it either be a weddin' or a wake! Listen, Mary, I'm standin' for the secretaryship of our Union. There's only one opposin' me; I'm popular with all the men, an' a good speaker— all are sayin' that I'll get elected.

MARY: Well?

JERRY: The job's worth three hundred and fifty pounds a year, Mary. You an' I could live nice and cosily on that; it would lift you out o' this place an' . . .

MARY: I haven't time to listen to you now—I have to go. (*She is going out when Jerry bars the way.*)

JERRY: (*appealingly*) Mary, what's come over you with me for the last few weeks? You hardly speak to me, an' then only a word with the face of bittherness on it. Have you forgotten, Mary, all the happy evenin's that were as sweet as the scented hawthorn that sheltered the sides o' the road as we sauntered through the country?

MARY: That's all over now. When you get your new job, Jerry, you won't be long findin' a girl far betther than I am for your sweetheart.

JERRY: Never, never, Mary! No matther what happens you'll always be the same to me.

MARY: I must be off; please let me go, Jerry.

JERRY: I'll go a bit o' the way with you.

MARY: You needn't, thanks; I want to be by meself.

JERRY: (*catching her arm*) You're goin' to meet another fella; you've clicked with someone else, me lady!

MARY: That's no concern o' yours, Jerry Devine; let me go!

JERRY: I saw yous comin' out o' the Cornflower Dance Class, an' you hangin' on his arm—a thin, lanky strip of a Micky Dazzler, with a walkin' stick and gloves!

VOICE OF JOHNNY: (*loudly*) What are you doin' there—pullin' about everything!

VOICE OF BOYLE: (*loudly and viciously*) I'm puttin' on me mole-skin trousers!

MARY: You're hurtin' me arm! Let me go, or I'll scream, an' then you'll have the oul' fella out on top of us!

JERRY: Don't be so hard on a fella, Mary, don't be so hard.

BOYLE: (*appearing at door*) What's the meanin' of all this hillabaloo?

MARY: Let me go, let me go!

BOYLE: D'ye hear me—what's all this hillabaloo about?

JERRY: (*plaintively*) Will you not give us one kind word, one kind word, Mary?

BOYLE: D'ye hear me talkin' to yous? What's all this hillabaloo for?

JERRY: Let me kiss your hand, your little, tiny, white hand!

BOYLE: Your little, tiny, white hand—are you takin' leave o' your senses, man?

(*Mary breaks away and rushes out.*)

BOYLE: This is nice goin's on in front of her father!

JERRY: Ah, dhry up, for God's sake! (*He follows Mary.*)

BOYLE: Chiselurs don't care a damn now about their parents, they're bringin' their fathers' greay hairs down with sorra to the grave, an' laughin' at it, laughin' at it. Ah, I suppose, it's just the same everywhere—the whole worl's in a state of chassis! (*He sits by the fire.*) Breakfast! Well, they can keep their breakfast for me. Not if they went down on their bended knees would I take it— I'll show them I've a little spirit left in me still! (*He goes over to the press, takes out a plate and looks at it.*) Sassige! Well, let her keep her sassige. (*He returns to the fire, takes up the teapot and gives it a gentle shake.*) The tay's wet right enough. (*A pause; he rises, goes to the press, takes out the sausage, puts it on the pan, and puts both on the fire. He attends the sausage with a fork.*)

BOYLE: (*singing*) When the robins nest agen,
And the flowers are in bloom,
When the Springtime's sunny smile seems to banish all sorrow
    an gloom;
Then me bonny blue-ey'd lad, if me heart be true till then—
He's promised he'll come back to me,
When the robins nest agen!

(*He lifts his head at the high note, and then drops his eyes to the pan.*)

BOYLE: (*singing*) When the . . .

(*Steps are heard approaching; he whips the pan off the fire and puts it under the bed, then sits down at the fire. The door opens and a bearded man looking in says*):

THE BEARDED MAN: You don't happen to want a sewin' machine?

BOYLE: (*furiously*) No, I don't want e'er a sewin' machine! (*He returns the pan to the fire, and commences to sing again.*)

BOYLE: (*singing*) When the robins nest agen,
And the flowers they are in bloom,
He's . . .

(*A thundering knock is heard at the street door.*)

BOYLE: There's a terrible tatheraraa—that's a stranger—that's nobody belongin' to the house. (*Another loud knock.*)

JOXER: (*sticking his head in at the door*) Did ye hear them tatherarahs?

BOYLE: Well, Joxer, I'm not deaf.

JOHNNY: (*appearing in his shirt and trousers at the door on left; his face is anxious and his voice is tremulous*): Who's that at the door; who's that at the door? Who gave that knock—d'yous hear me—are yous deaf or dhrunk or what?

BOYLE: (*to Johnny*) How the hell do I know who 'tis? Joxer, stick your head out o' the window an' see.

JOXER: An' mebbe get a bullet in the kisser? Ah, none o' them thricks for Joxer! It's betther to be a coward than a corpse!

BOYLE: (*looking cautiously out of the window*) It's a fella in a thrench coat.

JOHNNY: Holy Mary, Mother o' God, I . . .

BOYLE: He's goin' away—he must ha' got tired knockin'.

(*Johnny returns to the room on left.*)

BOYLE: Sit down an' have a cup of tay, Joxer.

JOXER: I'm afraid the missus ud pop in on us agen before we'd know where we are. Somethin's tellin' me to go at wanst.

BOYLE: Don't be superstitious, man; we're Dublin men, an' not boyos that's only afther comin' up from the bog o' Allen—though if she did come in, right enough, we'd be caught like rats in a thrap.

JOXER: An' you know the sort she is—she wouldn't listen to reason—an' wanse bitten twice shy.

BOYLE: (*going over to the window at back*) If the worst came to the worst, you could dart out here, Joxer; it's only a dhrop of a few feet to the roof of the return room, an' the first minute she goes into dh'other room, I'll give you the bend, an' you can slip in an' away.

JOXER: (*yielding to the temptation*) Ah, I won't stop very long, anyhow. (*Picking up a book from the table*) Whose is the buk?

BOYLE: Aw, one o' Mary's; she's always readin' lately—nothin' but thrash, too. There's one I was lookin' at dh'other day: three stories, The Doll's House, Ghosts, an' The Wild Duck —buks only fit for chiselurs!

JOXER: Didja ever rade *Elizabeth, or Th' Exile o' Sibayria* . . . ah, it's a darlin' story, a daarlin' story!

BOYLE: You eat your sassige, an' never min' *Th' Exile o' Sibayria*.

(*Both sit down; Boyle fills out tea, pours gravy on Joxer's plate and keeps the sausage for himself.*)

JOXER: What are you wearin' your moleskin trousers for?

BOYLE: I have to go to a job, Joxer. Just afther you'd gone Devine kem runnin' in to tell us that Father Farrell said if I went down to the job that's goin' on in Rathmines I'd get a start.

JOXER: Be the holy, that's good news!

BOYLE: How is it good news? I wondher if you were in my condition, would you call it good news?

JOXER: I thought . . .

BOYLE: You thought! You think too sudden sometimes, Joxer. D'ye know, I'm hardly able to crawl with the pains in me legs!

JOXER: Yis, yis; I forgot the pains in your legs. I know you can do nothing while they're at you.

BOYLE: You forgot; I don't think any of yous realize the state I'm in with the pains in me legs. What ud happen if I had to carry a bag o' cement?

JOXER: Ah, any man havin' the like of them pains id be down an' out, down an' out.

BOYLE: I wouldn't mind if he had said it to meself; but, no, oh no, he rushes in an' shouts it out in front o' Juno, an' you know what Juno is, Joxer. We all know Devine knows a little more than the rest of us, but he doesn't act as if he did; he's a good boy, sober, able to talk an' all that, but still . . .

JOXER: Oh ay; able to argufy, but still . . .

BOYLE: If he's runnin' afther Mary, aself, he's not goin' to be runnin' afther me. Captain Boyle's able to take care of himself.

Afther all, I'm not gettin' brought up on Virol. I never heard him usin' a curse; I don't believe he was ever dhrunk in his life—sure he's not like a Christian at all!

JOXER: You're afther takin' the word out o' me mouth—afther all, a Christian's natural, but he's unnatural.

BOYLE: His oul' fella was just the same—a Wicklow man.

JOXER: A Wicklow man! That explains the whole thing. I've met many a Wicklow man in me time, but I've never met wan that was any good.

BOYLE: 'Father Farrell,' says he, 'sent me down to tell you.' Father Farrell! . . . D'ye know, Joxer, I never like to be beholden to any o' the clergy.

JOXER: It's dangerous, right enough.

BOYLE: If they do anything for you, they'd want you to be livin' in the Chapel . . . I'm goin' to tell you somethin', Joxer, that I wouldn't tell to anybody else—the clergy always had too much power over the people in this unfortunate country.

JOXER: You could sing that if you had an air to it!

BOYLE: (*becoming enthusiastic*) Didn't they prevent the people in '47 from seizin' the corn, an' they starvin'; didn't they down Parnell; didn't they say that hell wasn't hot enough nor eternity long enough to punish the Fenians? We don't forget, we don't forget them things, Joxer. If they've taken everything else from us, Joxer, they've left us our memory.

JOXER: (*emotionally*) For mem'ry's the only friend that grief can call its own, that grief . . . can . . . call . . . its own!

BOYLE: Father Farrell's beginnin' to take a great interest in Captain Boyle; because of what Johnny did for his country, he says to me wan day. It's a curious way to reward Johnny be makin' his poor oul' father work. But, that's what the clergy want, Joxer—work, work, work for me an' you; havin' us mulin' from mornin' till night, so that they may be in betther fettle when they come hoppin' round for their dues! Job! Well, let him give his job to wan of his hymn-singin', prayer-spoutin', craw-thumpin' Confraternity men!

(*The voice of a coal-block vendor is heard chanting in the street.*)

VOICE OF COAL VENDOR: Blocks . . . coal-blocks! Blocks . . . coal-blocks!

JOXER: God be with the young days when you were steppin' the deck of a manly ship, with the win' blowin' a hurricane through the masts, an' the only sound you'd hear was, 'Port your helm!' an' the only answer, 'Port it is, sir!'

BOYLE: Them was the days, Joxer, them was the days. Nothin' was too hot or too heavy for me then. Sailin' from the Gulf o' Mexico to the Antarctic Ocean, I seen things, I seen things, Joxer, that no mortal man should speak about that knows his Catechism. Ofen an' ofen, when I was fixed to the wheel with a marlin-spike, an' the win's blowin' fierce an' the waves lashin' an' lashin', till you'd think every minute was goin' to be your last, an' it blowed, an' blowed—blew is the right word, Joxer, but blowed is what the sailors use . . .

JOXER: Aw, it's a darlin' word, a daarlin' word.

BOYLE: An', as it blowed an' blowed, I ofen looked up at the sky an' assed meself the question—what is the stars, what is the stars?

VOICE OF COAL VENDOR: Any blocks, coal-blocks; blocks, coal-blocks!

JOXER: Ah, that's the question, that's the question—what is the stars?

BOYLE: An' then, I'd have another look, an' I'd ass meself—what is the moon?

JOXER: Ah, that's the question—what is the moon, what is the moon?

(*Rapid steps are heard coming towards the door, Boyle makes desperate efforts to hide everything; Joxer rushes to the window in a frantic effort to get out; Boyle begins to innocently lilt— 'Oh, me darlin' Jennie, I will be thrue to thee', when the door is opened, and the black face of the coal vendor appears.*)

THE COAL VENDOR: D'yes want any blocks?

BOYLE: (*with a roar*) No, we don't want any blocks!

JOXER: (*coming back with a sigh of relief*) That's afther puttin' the heart across me—I could ha' sworn it was Juno. I'd betther be goin', Captain; you couldn't tell the minute Juno'd hop in on us.

BOYLE: Let her hop in; we may as well have it out first as at last. I've made up me mind—I'm not goin' to do only what she damn well likes.

JOXER: Them sentiments does you credit, Captain; I don't like to say anything as between man an' wife, but I say as a butty, as a butty, Captain, that you've stuck it too long, an' that it's about time you showed a little spunk.

How can man die betther than facin' fearful odds,
For th'ashes of his fathers an' the temples of his gods.

BOYLE: She has her rights—there's no one denyin' it, but haven't I me rights too?

JOXER: Of course you have—the sacred rights o' man!

BOYLE: Today, Joxer, there's goin' to be issued a proclamation be me, establishin' an independent Republic, an' Juno'll have to take an oath of allegiance.

JOXER: Be firm, be firm, Captain; the first few minutes'll be the worst: —if you gently touch a nettle it'll sting you for your pains; grasp it like a lad of mettle, an's as soft as silk remains!

VOICE OF JUNO OUTSIDE: Can't stop, Mrs. Madigan—I haven't a minute!

JOXER: (*flying out the window*) Holy God, here she is!

BOYLE: (*packing the things away with a rush in the press*) I knew that fella ud stop till she was in on top of us! (*He sits down by the fire.*)

(*June enters hastily; she is flurried and excited.*)

JUNO: Oh, you're in—you must have been only afther comin' in?

BOYLE: No, I never went out.

JUNO: It's curious, then, you never heard the knockin'. (*She puts her coat and hat on the bed.*)

BOYLE: Knockin'? Of course I heard the knockin'.

JUNO: An' why didn't you open the door, then? I suppose you were so busy with Joxer that you hadn't time.

BOYLE: I haven't seen Joxer since I seen him before. Joxer! What ud bring Joxer here?

JUNO: D'ye mean to tell me that the pair of yous wasn't collogin' together here when me back was turned?

BOYLE: What ud we be collogin' together about? I have somethin' else to think of besides collogin' with Joxer. I can swear on all the holy prayer books . . .

MRS. BOYLE: That you weren't in no snug! Go on in at wanst now an' take off that moleskin trousers o' yours, an' put on a collar an' tie to smarten yourself up a bit. There's a visitor comin' with Mary in a minute, an' he has great news for you.

BOYLE: A job, I suppose; let us get wan first before we start lookin' for another.

MRS. BOYLE: That's the thing that's able to put the win' up you. Well, it's no job, but news that'll give you the chance o' your life.

BOYLE: What's all the mystery about?

MRS. BOYLE: G'win an' take off the moleskin trousers when you're told!

(*Boyle goes into the room on left. Mrs. Boyle tidies up the room, puts the shovel under the bed, and goes to the press.*)

MRS. BOYLE: Oh, God bless us, looka the way everythin's thrun about! Oh, Joxer was here, Joxer was here!

(*Mary enters with Charlie Bentham; he is a young man of twenty-five, tall, good-looking, with a very high opinion of himself generally. He is dressed in a brown coat, brown knee-breeches, grey stockings, a brown sweater, with a deep blue tie; he carries gloves and a walking stick.*)

MRS. BOYLE: (*fussing round*) Come in, Mr. Bentham; sit down, Mr. Bentham, in this chair; it's more comfortabler than that, Mr. Bentham. Himself'll be here in a minute; he's just takin' off his trousers.

MARY: Mother!

BENTHAM: Please don't put yourself to any trouble, Mrs. Boyle. —I'm quite all right here, thank you.

MRS. BOYLE: An' to think of you knowin' Mary, an' she knowin' the news you had for us, an' wouldn't let on; but it's all the more welcomer now, for we were on our last lap!

VOICE OF JOHNNY INSIDE: What are you kickin' up all the racket for?

BOYLE: (*roughly*) I'm takin' off me moleskin trousers!

JOHNNY: Can't you do it, then, without lettin' the whole house know you're takin' off your trousers? What d'ye want puttin' them on an' takin' them off again?

BOYLE: Will you let me alone, will you let me alone? Am I never goin' to be done thryin' to please th' whole o' yous?

MRS. BOYLE: (*to Bentham*) You must excuse th' state o' th' place, Mr. Bentham; th' minute I turn me back that man o' mine always makes a litther o' th' place, a litther o' th' place.

BENTHAM: Don't worry, Mrs. Boyle; it's all right, I assure . . .

BOYLE: (*inside*) Where's me braces; where in th' name of God did I leave me braces . . . Ay, did you see where I put me braces?

JOHNNY: (*inside, calling out*) Ma, will you come in here an' take da away ou' o' this or he'll dhrive me mad.

MRS. BOYLE: (*going towards the door*) Dear, dear, dear, that man'll be lookin' for somethin' on th' day o' Judgement. (*Looking

into the room and calling to Boyle) Look at your braces, man, hangin'
round your neck!

BOYLE: (*inside*) Aw, Holy God!

MRS. BOYLE: (*calling*) Johnny, Johnny, come out here for a
minute.

JOHNNY: Oh, leave Johnny alone, an' don't be annoyin' him!

MRS. BOYLE: Come on, Johnny, till I inthroduce you to Mr.
Bentham. (*To Bentham*) Me son, Mr. Bentham; he's afther goin'
through the mill. He was only a chiselur of a Boy Scout in Easter
Week, when he got hit in the hip; and his arm was blew off in the
fight in O'Connell Street. (*Johnny comes in.*) Here he is, Mr.
Bentham; Mr. Bentham, Johnny. None can deny he done his bit
for Irelan', if that's goin' to do him any good.

JOHNNY: (*boastfully*) I'd do it agen, ma, I'd go it agen; for a
principle's a principle.

MRS. BOYLE: Ah, you lost your best principle, me boy, when you
lost your arm; them's the only sort o' principles that's any good to
a workin' man.

JOHNNY: Ireland only half free'll never be at peace while she
has a son left to pull a trigger.

MRS. BOYLE: To be sure, to be sure—no bread's a lot betther
than half a loaf. (*Calling loudly to Boyle.*) Will you hurry up there?
(*Boyle enters in his best trousers, which aren't too good, and
looks very uncomfortable in his collar and tie.*)

MRS. BOYLE: This is me husband; Mr. Boyle, Mr. Bentham.

BENTHAM: Ah, very glad to know you, Mr. Boyle. How are you?

BOYLE: Ah, I'm not too well at all; I suffer terrible with pains
in me legs. Juno can tell you there what . . .

MRS. BOYLE: You won't have many pains in your legs when
you hear what Mr. Bentham has to tell you.

BENTHAM: Juno! What an interesting name! It reminds one
of Homer's glorious story of ancient gods and heroes.

BOYLE: Yis, doesn't it? You see, Juno was born an' christened
in June; I met her in June; we were married in June, an' Johnny
was born in June, so wan day I says to her, 'You should ha' been
called Juno,' an' the name stuck to her ever since.

MRS. BOYLE: Here, we can talk o' them things agen; let Mr.
Bentham say what he has to say now.

BENTHAM: Well, Mr. Boyle, I suppose you'll remember a
Mr. Ellison of Santry—he's a relative of yours, I think.

BOYLE: (*viciously*) Is it that prognosticator an' procrastinator! Of course I remember him.

BENTHAM: Well, he's dead, Mr. Boyle . . .

BOYLE: Sorra many'll go into mournin' for him.

MRS. BOYLE: Wait till you hear what Mr. Bentham has to say, and then, maybe, you'll change your opinion.

BENTHAM: A week before he died he sent for me to write his will for him. He told me that there were two only that he wished to leave his property to: his second cousin Michael Finnegan of Santry, and John Boyle, his first cousin of Dublin.

BOYLE: (*excitedly*) Me, is it me, me?

BENTHAM: You, Mr. Boyle; I'll read a copy of the will that I have here with me, which has been duly filed in the Court of Probate. (*He takes a paper from his pocket and reads.*)

6th February, 1922.

This is the last Will and Testament of William Ellison, of Santry, in the County of Dublin. I hereby order and wish my property to be sold and divided as follows:

£20 to the St. Vincent De Paul Society.

£60 for Masses for the repose of my soul (5s. for each Mass).

The rest of my property to be divided between my first and second cousins.

I hereby appoint Timothy Buckly of Santry, and Hugh Brierly, of Coolock, to be my Executors.

(Signed) William Ellison, Hugh Brierly, Timothy Buckly, Charles Bentham, N.T.

BOYLE: (*eagerly*) An' how much'll be comin' out of it, Mr. Bentham?

BENTHAM: The Executors told me that half of the property would be anything between £1,500 and £2,000.

MARY: A fortune, father, a fortune!

JOHNNY: We'll be able to get out o' this place now, an' go somewhere we're not known.

MRS. BOYLE: You won' have to trouble about a job for a while, Jack.

BOYLE: (*fervently*) I'll never doubt the goodness o' God agen.

BENTHAM: I congratulate you, Mr. Boyle. (*They shake hands.*)

BOYLE: An' now, Mr. Bentham, you'll have to have a wet.

BENTHAM: A wet?

BOYLE: A wet—a jar—a boul!

MRS. BOYLE: Jack, you're speakin' to Mr. Bentham, an' not to Joxer.

BOYLE: (*solemnly*) Juno . . . Mary . . . Johnny . . . we'll have to go into mournin' at wanst . . . I never expected that poor Bill ud die so sudden . . . Well, we all have to die some day . . . you, Juno, today . . . an' me, maybe, tomorrow . . . It's sad, but it can't be helped . . . Requiescat in pace . . . or, usin' our oul' tongue like St. Patrick or St. Briget, Guh sayeree jeea ayera!

MARY: Oh, father, that's not Rest in Peace; that's God save Ireland.

BOYLE: U-u-ugh, it's all the same—isn't it a prayer? . . . Juno, I'm done with Joxer; he's nothin' but a prognosticator an' a . . .

JOXER: (*climbing angrily through the window and bounding into the room*) You're done with Joxer, are you? Maybe you thought I'd stop on the roof all the night for you! Joxer out on the roof with the win' blowin' through him was nothin' to you an' your friend with the collar an' tie!

MRS. BOYLE: What in the name o' God brought you out on the roof; what were you doin' there?

JOXER: (*ironically*) I was dhreamin' I was standin' on the bridge of a ship, an' she sailin' the Antarctic Ocean, an' it blowed an' blowed, an' I lookin' up at the sky an' sayin', what is the stars, what is the stars?

MRS. BOYLE: (*opening the door and standing at it*) Here, get ou' o' this, Joxer Daly; I was always thinkin' you had a slate off.

JOXER: (*moving to the door*) I have to laugh every time I look at the deep sea sailor; an' a row on a river ud make him seasick!

BOYLE: Get ou' o' this before I take the law into me own hands!

JOXER: (*going out*) Say aw rewaeawr, but not good-bye. Lookin' for work, an' prayin' to God he won't get it! (*He goes.*)

MRS. BOYLE: I'm tired tellin' you what Joxer was; maybe now you see yourself the kind he is.

BOYLE: He'll never blow the froth off a pint o' mine agen, that's a sure thing. Johnny . . . Mary . . . you're to keep yourselves to yourselves for the future. Juno, I'm done with Joxer . . . I'm a new man from this out . . . (*Clasping Juno's hand, and singing emotionally.*)

Oh, me darlin' Juno, I will be thrue to thee;
Me own, me darlin' Juno, you're all the world to me.

DEATH OF A SALESMAN

(An excerpt from Act II)

by

Arthur Miller

CHARACTERS

STANLEY, *a waiter*.
WILLY LOMAN, *the salesman*.
BIFF ⎱ *his sons.*
HAPPY ⎰
THE GIRL (MISS FORSYTHE).
LETTA.
LINDA, *Willy's wife*.
YOUNG BERNARD.
THE WOMAN (*an off-stage voice*).

THE AUTHOR

Arthur Miller was born in New York and is widely regarded as one of the most important of living dramatists. In his youth he worked at a large number of manual jobs and then studied playwriting at the University of Michigan. His first major success was *All My Sons* after World War II, and this was followed by *Death of a Salesman* in 1949, then *The Crucible* and *A View from the Bridge*. He has also written film scripts, in particular *The Misfits*, which marked the last screen appearance of his late wife, Marilyn Monroe.

THE PLAY

Death of a Salesman is considered by many to be the only genuine
tragedy written in the twentieth century, although others disagree,
claiming that Willy Loman is too small a man to be a true tragic
hero. Nevertheless, we can agree that it is a most moving drama,
if not a tragedy.

Willy is the typical small man of modern materialist society.
He has lived on hope all his life—hope that he might pull off the
'big deal', hope that his luck might change. He is obsessed with
success, in a worldly sense, and he fails to see the arid nature of his
own life. His advice to his boys is that they should not just be liked,
they should be *well* liked. His tragedy stems from the failure
of his favourite son, Biff, who began as a school football
hero and seemed to have the world at his feet. Biff is now
thirty-five, and what the Americans call 'a bum'. He has
returned home, however, for a final attempt to make something of
himself. He is encouraged by Willy to go to see Oliver, a big
business man, in an attempt to get him to back some vague business
venture, but Biff steals Oliver's fountain pen and it all comes to
nothing. In the meantime, Willy has been showing evidence that
his mind is affected. He drifts from the present to the past and
seems unable to distinguish between them. He holds imaginary
conversations with his dead brother, Ben, who made a fortune
before he was twenty-one. Finally, Willy hits on a scheme to help
the boys—he will commit suicide and leave them his insurance

money, so he drives off with 'Ben' sitting beside him and has a fatal car crash. The point may be summed up in one of the final speeches in the play: 'Willy was a salesman. And for a salesman, there is no rock bottom to the life. He don't put a bolt to a nut, he don't tell you the law or give you medicine. He's a man way out there in the blue, riding on a smile and a shoeshine. And when they start not smiling back—that's an earthquake . . . A salesman is got to dream, boy. It comes with the territory.'

The scene included here occurs in a restaurant. Willy's two boys, Biff and Happy, are taking him out to dinner to celebrate the success they are all sure Biff will have with Oliver.

DEATH OF A SALESMAN

An excerpt from Act II

(The scene in this excerpt is a restaurant on the forestage area. Behind it is the Loman house, unlit when the scene begins.)
Suddenly raucous music is heard, and a red glow rises on this fore-stage area. Stanley, a young waiter, appears carrying a table, followed by Happy, who is carrying two chairs.

STANLEY: (*putting the table down*) That's all right, Mr. Loman, I can handle it myself. (*He turns and takes the chairs from Happy and places them at the table.*)

HAPPY: (*glancing around*) Oh, this is better.

STANLEY: Sure, in the front there you're in the middle of all kinds a noise. Whenever you got a party, Mr. Loman, you just tell me and I'll put you back here. Y'know, there's a lotta people they don't like it private, because when they go out they like to see a lotta action around them because they're sick and tired to stay in the house by theirself. But I know you, you ain't from Hacken-sack. You know what I mean?

HAPPY: (*sitting down*) So how's it coming, Stanley?

STANLEY: Ah, it's a dog's life. I only wish during the war they'd a took me in the Army. I coulda been dead by now.

HAPPY: My brother's back, Stanley.

STANLEY: Oh, he come back, heh? From the Far West.

HAPPY: Yeah, big cattle man, my brother, so treat him right. And my father's coming too.

STANLEY: Oh, your father too!

HAPPY: You got a couple of nice lobsters?

STANLEY: Hundred per cent, big.

HAPPY: I want them with the claws.

STANLEY: Don't worry, I don't give you no mice. (*Happy laughs.*) How about some wine? It'll put a head on the meal.

HAPPY: No. You remember, Stanley, that recipe I brought you from overseas? With the champagne in it?

STANLEY: Oh, yeah, sure. I still got it tacked up yet in the kitchen. But that'll have to cost a buck a piece anyways.

HAPPY: That's all right.

STANLEY: What'd you, hit a number or somethin'?

HAPPY: No, it's a little celebration. My brother is—I think he pulled off a big deal today. I think we're going into business together.

STANLEY: Great! That's the best for you. Because a family business, you know what I mean?—that's the best.

HAPPY: That's what I think.

STANLEY: 'Cause what's the difference? Somebody steals? It's in the family. You know what I mean? (*Sotto voce*) Like this bartender here. The boss is goin' crazy what kinda leak he's got in the cash register. You put it in but it don't come out.

HAPPY: (*raising his head*) Sh!

STANLEY: What?

HAPPY: You notice I wasn't lookin' right or left, was I?

STANLEY: No.

HAPPY: And my eyes are closed.

STANLEY: So what's the—?

HAPPY: Strudel's comin'.

(*Stanley, catching on, looks round.*)

STANLEY: Ah, no, there's no—

(*He breaks off as a furred, lavishly dressed girl enters and sits at the next table. Both follow her with their eyes.*)

STANLEY: Geez, how'd ya know?

HAPPY: I got radar or something. (*Staring directly at her profile*) Oooooooo . . . Stanley.

STANLEY: I think that's for you, Mr. Loman.

HAPPY: Look at that mouth. Oh God. And the binoculars.

STANLEY: Geez, you got a life, Mr. Loman.

HAPPY: Wait on her.

STANLEY: (*going to the girl's table*) Would you like a menu, ma'am?

GIRL: I'm expecting someone, but I'd like a—

HAPPY: Why don't you bring her—excuse me, miss, do you mind? I sell champagne, and I'd like you to try my brand. Bring her a champagne, Stanley.

GIRL: That's awfully nice of you.

HAPPY: Don't mention it. It's all company money. (*He laughs.*)

GIRL: That's a charming product to be selling, isn't it?

HAPPY: Oh, gets to be like everything else. Selling is selling, y'know.

GIRL: I suppose.

HAPPY: You don't happen to sell, do you?

GIRL: No, I don't sell.

HAPPY: Would you object to a compliment from a stranger? You ought to be on a magazine cover.

GIRL: (*looking at him a little archly*) I have been.

(*Stanley comes in with a glass of champagne.*)

HAPPY: What'd I say before, Stanley? You see? She's a cover girl.

STANLEY: Oh, I could see, I could see.

HAPPY: (*to the girl*) What magazine?

GIRL: Oh, a lot of them. (*She takes the drink.*) Thank you.

HAPPY: You know what they say in France, don't you? 'Champagne is the drink of the complexion'—Hya, Biff!

(*Biff has entered and sits with Happy.*)

BIFF: Hello, kid. Sorry I'm late.

HAPPY: I just got here. Uh, Miss—?

GIRL: Forsythe.

HAPPY: Miss Forsythe, this is my brother.

BIFF: Is Dad here?

HAPPY: His name is Biff. You might have heard of him. Great football player.

GIRL: Really? What team?

HAPPY: Are you familiar with football?

GIRL: No, I'm afraid I'm not.

HAPPY: Biff is quarterback with the New York Giants..

GIRL: Well, that is nice, isn't it? (*She drinks.*)

HAPPY: Good health.

GIRL: I'm happy to meet you.

HAPPY: That's my name. Hap. It's really Harold, but at West Point they called me Happy.

GIRL: (*now really impressed*) Oh, I see. How do you do? (*She turns her profile.*)

BIFF: Isn't Dad coming?

HAPPY: You want her?

BIFF: Oh, I could never make that.

HAPPY: I remember the time that idea would never come into your head. Where's the old confidence, Biff?

BIFF: I just saw Oliver—

HAPPY: Wait a minute. I've got to see that old confidence again. Watch this. (*Turning to the girl*) Honey? (*She turns to him.*) Are you busy?

GIRL: Well, I am . . . but I could make a phone call.

HAPPY: Do that, will you, honey? And see if you can get a friend. We'll be here for a while. Biff is one of the greatest football players in the country.

GIRL: (*standing up*) Well, I'm certainly happy to meet you.

HAPPY: Come back soon.

GIRL: I'll try.

HAPPY: Don't try, honey, try hard.

(*The girl exits. Stanley follows, shaking his head in bewildered admiration.*)

HAPPY: Isn't that a shame now? A beautiful girl like that? That's why I can't get married. There's not a good woman in a thousand. New York is loaded with them, kid!

BIFF: (*strangely unnerved*) Cut it out, will ya? I want to say something to you.

HAPPY: Did you see Oliver?

BIFF: I saw him all right. Now look, I want to tell Dad a couple of things and I want you to help me.

HAPPY: What? Is he going to back you?

BIFF: Are you crazy? You're out of your goddam head, you know that?

HAPPY: Why? What happened?

BIFF: (*breathlessly*) I did a terrible thing today, Hap. It's been the strangest day I ever went through. I'm all numb, I swear.

HAPPY: You mean he wouldn't see you?

BIFF: Well, I waited six hours for him, see? All day. Kept sending my name in. Even tried to date his secretary so she'd get me to him, but no soap.

HAPPY: Because you're not showin' the old confidence, Biff. He remembered you, didn't he?

BIFF: (*stopping Happy with a gesture*) Finally, about five o'clock, he comes out. Didn't remember who I was or anything. I felt such an idiot, Hap.

HAPPY: Did you tell him my Florida idea?

BIFF: He walked away. I saw him for one minute. I got so mad I could've torn the walls down! How the hell did I ever get the idea I was a salesman there? I even believed myself that I'd been a salesman for him! And then he gave me one look and—I realized what a ridiculous lie my whole life has been! We've been talking in a dream for fifteen years. I was a shipping clerk.

HAPPY: What'd you do?

BIFF: (*with great tension and wonder*) Well, he left, see. And the secretary went out. I was all alone in the waiting-room. I don' know what come over me, Hap. The next thing I know I'm in his office—panelled walls, everything. I can't explain it. I—Hap, I took his fountain pen.

HAPPY: Geez, did he catch you?

BIFF: I ran out. I ran down all eleven flights. I ran and ran and ran.

HAPPY: That was an awful dumb—what'd you do that for?

BIFF: (*agonized*) I don't know, I just—wanted to take something, I don't know. You gotta help me, Hap, I'm gonna tell Pop.

HAPPY: You crazy? What for?

BIFF: Hap, he's got to understand that I'm not the man somebody lends that kind of money to. He thinks I've been spiting him all these years and it's eating him up.

HAPPY: That's just it. You tell him something nice.

BIFF: I can't.

HAPPY: Say you got a lunch date with Oliver tomorrow.

BIFF: So what do I do tomorrow?

HAPPY: You leave the house tomorrow and come back at night and say Oliver is thinking it over. And he thinks it over for a couple of weeks, and gradually it fades away and nobody's the worse.

BIFF: But it'll go on forever!

HAPPY: Dad is never so happy as when he's looking forward to something.

(*Willy enters.*)

HAPPY: Hello, scout!

WILLY: Gee, I haven't been here in years!

(*Stanley has followed Willy in and sets a chair for him. Stanley starts off but Happy stops him.*)

HAPPY: Stanley!

(*Stanley stands by, waiting for an order.*)

BIFF: (*going to Willy with guilt, as to an invalid*) Sit down, Pop. You want a drink?

WILLY: Sure, I don't mind.

BIFF: Let's get a load on.

WILLY: You look worried.

BIFF: N-no. (*To Stanley*) Scotch all round. Make it doubles.

STANLEY: Doubles, right. (*He goes.*)

WILLY: You had a couple already, didn't you?

BIFF: Just a couple, yeah.

WILLY: Well, what happened, boy? (*Nodding affirmatively, with a smile*) Everything go all right?

BIFF: (*takes a breath, then reaches out and grasps Willy's hand*) Pal . . . (*He is smiling bravely, and Willy is smiling too.*) I had an experience today.

HAPPY: Terrific, Pop.

WILLY: That so? What happened?

BIFF: (*high, slightly alcoholic, above the earth*) I'm going to tell you everything from the first to last. It's been a strange day. (*Silence. He looks around, composes himself as best he can, but his breath keeps breaking the rhythm of his voice.*) I had to wait quite a while for him, and—

WILLY: Oliver?

BIFF: Yeah, Oliver. All day, as a matter of cold fact. And a lot of—instances—facts, Pop, facts about my life came back to me. Who was it, Pop? Who ever said I was a salesman with Oliver?

WILLY: Well, you were.

BIFF: No, Dad, I was a shipping clerk.

WILLY: But you were practically—

BIFF: (*with determination*) Dad, I don't know who said it first, but I was never a salesman for Bill Oliver.

WILLY: What're you talking about?

BIFF: Let's hold to the facts tonight, Pop. I was a shipping clerk.

WILLY: (*angrily*) All right, now listen to me—

BIFF: Why don't you let me finish?

WILLY: I'm not interested in stories about the past or anything of that kind because the woods are burning, boys, you understand? There's a big blaze going on all around. I was fired today.

BIFF: (*shocked*) How could you be?

WILLY: I was fired, and I'm looking for a little good news to tell your mother, because the woman has waited and the woman has suffered. The gist of it is that I haven't got a story left in my

head, Biff. So don't give me a lecture about facts and aspects.
I am not interested. Now what've you got to say to me?

(*Stanley enters with three drinks. They wait until he leaves.*)

WILLY: Did you see Oliver?

BIFF: Jesus, Dad!

WILLY: You mean you didn't go up there?

HAPPY: Sure he went up there.

BIFF: I did. I—saw him. How could they fire you?

WILLY: (*on the edge of his chair*) What kind of a welcome did
he give you?

BIFF: He won't even let you work on commission?

WILLY: I'm out. (*Driving*) So tell me, he gave you a warm
welcome?

HAPPY: Sure, Pop, sure!

BIFF: (*driven*) Well, it was kind of—

WILLY: I was wondering if he'd remember you. (*To Happy*)
Imagine, man doesn't see him for ten, twelve years and gives him
that kind of welcome!

HAPPY: Damn right!

BIFF: (*trying to return to the offensive*) Pop, look—

WILLY: You know why he remembered you, don't you?
Because you impressed him in those days.

BIFF: Let's talk quietly and get this down to the facts, huh?

WILLY: (*as though Biff had been interrupting*) Well, what happened? It's great news, Biff. Did he take you into his office or'd
you talk in the waiting-room?

BIFF: Well, he came in, see, and—

WILLY: (*with a big smile*) What'd he say? Betcha he threw his
arm around you.

BIFF: Well, he kinda—

WILLY: He's a fine man. (*To Happy*) Very hard man to see,
y'know.

HAPPY: (*agreeing*) Oh, I know.

WILLY: (*to Biff*) Is that where you had the drinks?

BIFF: Yeah, he gave me a couple of—no, no!

HAPPY: (*cutting in*) He told him my Florida idea.

WILLY: Don't interrupt. (*To Biff*) How'd he react to the
Florida idea?

BIFF: Dad, will you give me a minute to explain?

WILLY: I've been waiting for you to explain since I sat down here! What happened? He took you into his office and what?

BIFF: Well—I talked. And—he listened, see.

WILLY: Famous for the way he listens, y'know. What was his answer?

BIFF: His answer was—(*He breaks off, suddenly angry.*) Dad, you're not letting me tell you what I want to tell you!

WILLY: (*accusing, angered*) You didn't see him, did you?

BIFF: I did see him!

WILLY: What'd you insult him or something? You insulted him, didn't you?

BIFF: Listen, will you let me out of it, will you just let me out of it!

HAPPY: What the hell!

WILLY: Tell me what happened!

BIFF: (*to Happy*) I can't talk to him!

(*A single, raw trumpet note jars the ear, and instantly the Loman house which has remained visible behind the little restaurant area, but in relative darkness—the house comes alive as it is, stained with greenish leaves as though seen through the murk of a memory. And while Biff and Happy are talking with Willy in the restaurant, we glimpse Willy's thought of young Bernard, dressed in knickers as he used to be, rushing into the kitchen and calling.*)

YOUNG BERNARD: (*frantically*) Mrs. Loman, Mrs. Loman!

HAPPY: Tell him what happened!

BIFF: (*to Happy*) Shut up and leave me alone!

WILLY: No, no! You had to go and flunk math!

BIFF: What math? What're you talking about?

YOUNG BERNARD: Mrs. Loman, Mrs. Loman!

(*Linda appears in the house, as of old.*)

WILLY: (*wildly*) Math, math, math!

BIFF: Take it easy, Pop!

YOUNG BERNARD: Mrs. Loman!

WILLY: (*furiously*) If you hadn't flunked you'd've been set by now!

BIFF: Now, look, I'm gonna tell you what happened, and you're going to listen to me.

YOUNG BERNARD: Mrs. Loman!

BIFF: I waited six hours—

HAPPY: What the hell are you saying?

BIFF: I kept sending my name in but he wouldn't see me. So finally he . . . (*He continues unheard as the light fades low on the restaurant, and our total attention is on the house.*)

YOUNG BERNARD: Biff flunked math!

LINDA: No!

YOUNG BERNARD: Birnbaum flunked him! They won't graduate him!

LINDA: But they have to. He's gotta go to the University. Where is he? Biff! Biff!

YOUNG BERNARD: No, he left. He went to Grand Central.

LINDA: Grand—you mean he went to Boston!

YOUNG BERNARD: Is Uncle Willy in Boston?

LINDA: Oh, maybe Willy can talk to the teacher. Oh, the poor, poor boy!

(*The light on Bernard and Linda suddenly snaps out, and we are back in the restaurant where Biff, who has been 'talking' throughout this imagined scene, now becomes audible to us. He is holding up a fountain pen, and Willy is staring at him as though desperately trying to focus his mind on what his son is saying.*)

BIFF: . . . so I'm washed up with Oliver, you understand? Are you listening to me?

WILLY: (*at a loss*) Yeah, sure. If you hadn't flunked—

BIFF: Flunked what? What're you talking about?

WILLY: Don't blame everything on me! I didn't flunk math—you did! What pen?

HAPPY: That was awful dumb, Biff, a pen like that is worth—

WILLY: (*seeing the pen for the first time*) You took Oliver's pen?

BIFF: (*weakening*) Dad, I just explained it to you.

WILLY: You stole Bill Oliver's fountain pen!

BIFF: I didn't exactly steal it! That's just what I've been explaining to you!

HAPPY: He had it in his hand and just then Oliver walked in, so he got nervous and stuck it in his pocket!

WILLY: My God, Biff!

BIFF: I never intended to do it, Dad!

(*Oh the heels of Biff's shout we hear, as though out of the air, the phone-distorted voice of a hotel switchboard operator.*)

OPERATOR'S VOICE: Standish Arms, good evening!

WILLY: (*shouting wildly into the air*) I'm not in my room!

BIFF: (*frightened*) Dad, what's the matter? (*He and Happy stand up.*)

OPERATOR: Ringing Mr. Loman for you!

WILLY: I'm not there, stop it!

BIFF: (*horrified, gets down on one knee before Willy*) Dad, I'll make good, I'll make good. (*Willy tries to get to his feet. Biff holds him down.*) Sit down now.

WILLY: No, you're no good, you're no good for anything.

BIFF: I am, Dad, I'll find something else, you understand? Now don't worry about anything. (*He holds up Willy's face.*) Talk to me, Dad.

OPERATOR: Mr. Loman does not answer, Shall I page him?

WILLY: (*attempting to stand, as though to rush and silence the operator*) No, no, no!

HAPPY: He'll strike something, Pop!

WILLY: No, no . . .

BIFF: (*desperately, standing over Willy*) Pop, listen! Listen to me! I'm telling you something good. Oliver talked to his partner about the Florida idea. You listening? He--he talked to his partner, and he came to me . . . I'm going to be all right, you hear? Dad, listen to me, he said it was just a question of the amount!

WILLY: Then you . . . got it?

HAPPY: He's gonna be terrific, Pop!

WILLY: (*trying to stand*) Then you got it, haven't you? You got it! You got it!

BIFF: (*agonized, holds Willy down*) No, no. Look, Pop. I'm supposed to have lunch with them tomorrow. I'm just telling you this so you'll know that I can still make an impression, Pop. And I'll make good somewhere, but I can't go tomorrow, see?

WILLY: Why not? You simply—

BIFF: But the pen, Pop!

WILLY: You give it to him and tell him it was an oversight!

HAPPY: Sure, have lunch tomorrow!

BIFF: I can't say that—

WILLY: You were doing a crossword puzzle and accidentally used his pen!

BIFF: Listen, kid, I took those balls years ago, now I walk in with his fountain pen? That clinches it, don't you see? I can't face him like that! I'll try elsewhere.

PAGE'S VOICE: Paging Mr. Loman!

WILLY: Don't you want to be anything?

BIFF: Pop, how can I go back?

WILLY: You don't want to be anything, is that what's behind it?

BIFF: (*now angry at Willy for not crediting his sympathy*) Don't take it that way! You think it was easy walking into that office after what I'd done to him? A team of horses couldn't have dragged me back to Bill Oliver!

WILLY: Then why'd you go?

BIFF: Why did I go? Why did I go! Look at you! Look at what's become of you!

(*Willy hears the laughter of the woman and his head turns.*)

WILLY: Biff, you're going to go to that lunch tomorrow, or—

BIFF: I can't go. I've got no appointment!

HAPPY: Biff, for . . .!

WILLY: Are you spiting me?

BIFF: Don't take it that way! Goddammit!

WILLY: (*strikes Biff and falters away from the table*) You rotten little louse! Are you spiting me?

THE WOMAN'S VOICE: Someone's at the door, Willy!

BIFF: I'm no good, can't you see what I am?

HAPPY: (*separating them*) Hey, you're in a restaurant! Now cut it out, both of you! (*The girls enter.*) Hello, girls, sit down.

(*The woman's laughter is heard again.*)

MISS FORSYTHE: I guess we might as well. This is Letta.

THE WOMAN'S VOICE: Willy, are you going to wake up?

BIFF: (*ignoring Willy*) How're ya, miss, sit down. What do you drink?

MISS FORSYTHE: Letta might not be able to stay long.

LETTA: I gotta get up very early tomorrow. I got jury duty. I'm so excited! Were you fellows ever on a jury?

BIFF: No, but I been in front of them! (*The girls laugh.*) This is my father.

LETTA: Isn't he cute? Sit down with us, Pop.

HAPPY: Sit him down, Biff!

BIFF: (*going to him*) Come on, slugger, drink us under the table. To hell with it! Come on, sit down, pal.

(*On Biff's insistence, Willy is about to sit.*)

THE WOMAN'S VOICE: (*now urgently*) Willy, are you going to answer that door?

(*The woman's call pulls Willy back. He starts left, befuddled.*)

BIFF: Hey, where are you going?

WILLY: Open the door.

BIFF: The door?

WILLY: The washroom . . . the door . . . where's the door?

BIFF: (*leading Willy to the right*) Just go straight down. (*Willy moves right.*)

THE WOMAN'S VOICE: Willy, Willy, are you going to get up, get up, get up, get up? (*Willy exits right.*)

LETTA: I think it's sweet you bring your daddy along.

MISS FORSYTHE: Oh, he isn't really your father!

BIFF: (*at left, turning to her resentfully*) Miss Forsythe, you've just seen a prince walk by. A fine, troubled prince. A hard-working, unappreciated prince. A pal, you understand? A good companion. Always for his boys.

LETTA: That's so sweet.

HAPPY: Well, girls, what's the programme? We're wasting time. Come on, Biff. Gather round. Where would you like to go?

BIFF: Why don't you do something for him?

HAPPY: Me!

BIFF: Don't you give a damn for him, Hap?

HAPPY: What're you talking about? I'm the one who—

BIFF: I sense it, you don't give a goddam about him. (*He takes the rolled up hose from his pocket and puts it on the table in front of Happy.*) Look what I found in the cellar, for Christ's sake. How can you bear to let it go on?

HAPPY: Me? Who goes away? Who runs off and—

BIFF: Yeah, but he doesn't mean anything to you. You could help him—I can't! Don't you understand what I'm talking about? He's going to kill himself, don't you know that?

HAPPY: Don't I know it! Me!

BIFF: Hap, help him! Jesus . . . help him . . . Help me, help me, I can't bear to look at his face! (*Ready to weep, he hurries out, up right.*)

HAPPY: (*starting after him*) Where are you going?

MISS FORSYTHE: What's he so mad about?

HAPPY: Come on, girls, we'll catch up with him.

MISS FORSYTHE: (*as Happy pushes her out*) Say, I don't like that temper of his!

HAPPY: He's just a little overstrung, he'll be all right.

WILLY: (*off left, as the woman laughs*) Don't answer! Don't answer!

LETTA: Don't you want to tell your father—

HAPPY: No, that's not my father. He's just a guy. Come on, we'll catch Biff, and, honey, we're going to paint this town! Stanley, where's the check! Hey, Stanley!

(*They exit. Stanley looking toward left.*)

STANLEY: (*calling to Happy indignantly*) Mr. Loman! Mr. Loman!

The Epic Theatre of Germany

THE CAUCASIAN CHALK CIRCLE

(*Excerpts from Part II*)

by

Bertolt Brecht

CHARACTERS

THE STORY TELLER.
AZDAK, *a village recorder who has been made a judge.*
SHAUWA, *a village policeman who has been made public prosecutor*
AN INVALID.
A DOCTOR.
A LIMPING MAN.
A BLACKMAILER.
FIRST RICH FARMER.
SECOND RICH FARMER.
THIRD RICH FARMER.
AN OLD PEASANT WOMAN.
A BANDIT.
SEVERAL VILLAGERS.
SEVERAL IRONSHIRT GUARDS.
THE CHILD, MICHAEL.
GRUSHA, *a kitchen maid, foster mother of Michael.*
THE GOVERNOR'S COOK.
THE GOVERNOR'S WIFE, *natural mother of Michael.*
THE FIRST LAWYER.
THE SECOND LAWYER.
SIMON, *engaged to Grusha.*
A DESPATCH RIDER.
A CORPORAL.
AN OLD MAN.
AN OLD WOMAN.

THE AUTHOR

Bertolt Brecht was born in Germany in 1898. He came from a fairly well-to-do family who gave him a good education. He entered the University of Munich in 1917 to study medicine, but did not finish this as he was called up for military service in the First World War. The experiences of this left him with a hatred of war and a sense of its futility. In the confused and troubled years that Germany went through after the war, he emerged as a dramatist whose plays had a strong social message. During the Hitler regime he had to flee his country and took refuge in the U.S.A. After the Second World War he returned, and continued to write and produce plays until his death in 1956. In these later years he was connected with the famous Berlin Ensemble Theatre.

Brecht wrote a great number of plays, some mere propaganda, but some which seem to be enduring. It is generally considered that his best plays are *Mother Courage, The Life of Galileo, The Good Woman of Setzuan* and *The Caucasian Chalk Circle*.

THE PLAY

The Caucasian Chalk Circle has two plots and the narrative is told, as in most of Brecht's plays, in a large number of short scenes. The first plot concerns a peasant girl Grusha who saves the baby son of a governor during a revolution in which the governor is

killed and his selfish and pleasure-loving wife abandons the child. Grusha goes through many adventures and hardships in her flight with the child, but she manages to care for it and grows to love it. The other plot concerns a rascal of a peasant called Azdak whom the soldiers of the country make a judge as a sort of joke. He goes off on a rampaging procession through the countryside, delivering judgements that completely reverse accepted standards of justice. He accepts bribes, the trials he holds are farcical, he dispenses 'justice'. In these satirical scenes Brecht is seeking to make his audiences think about the real processes of justice. The soldiers, tiring of their joke, prepare to hang Azdak, but he is saved by a message from the Grand Duke, whose life Azdak had saved earlier in the revolution. The Grand Duke now appoints him as a real judge, and in his next case the two plots come together. Azdak has to sit in judgement on the case of the late Governor's wife v. the peasant girl Grusha for the custody of the child. Grusha loves it; the Governor's wife wants it back so that she can get control of her late husband's estates. This trial is the final scene in the extract we have chosen.

THE CAUCASIAN CHALK CIRCLE

Excerpts from Part II

The scene is the Court of Justice in a Caucasian city. Azdak, a village recorder, is dressed in a judge's gown and is sitting in the judge's chair, peeling an apple. Shauwa, a village policeman, is sweeping out the hall. On one side there is an invalid in a wheelchair. Opposite, there is a young man accused of blackmail. An Ironshirt stands on guard, holding the Ironshirts' banner.

AZDAK: In consideration of the large number of cases, the Court today will hear two cases at a time. Before I open the proceedings, a short announcement—I accept—(*He stretches out his hand. The Blackmailer is the only one to produce any money. He hands it to Azdak.*)—I reserve for myself the right to punish one of the parties here for contempt of court. (*He glances at the invalid.*) You (*to the Doctor*) are a doctor, and you (*to the invalid*) are bringing a complaint against him. Is the doctor responsible for your condition?

THE INVALID: Yes. I had a stroke because of him.

AZDAK: That would be professional negligence.

THE INVALID: More than negligence. I gave this man money for his studies. So far, he hasn't paid me back a cent. And when I heard he was treating a patient free, I had a stroke.

AZDAK: Rightly. (*To a limping man*) And you, what do you want here?

THE LIMPING MAN: I'm the patient, your honour.

AZDAK: He treated your leg for nothing?

THE LIMPING MAN: The wrong leg! My rheumatism was in the left leg, and he operated on the right. That's why I limp now.

AZDAK: And you got it free?

THE INVALID: A five-hundred-piastre operation free! For nothing! For a God-bless-you! And I paid for this man's studies! (*To the Doctor*) Did they teach you to operate free?

THE DOCTOR: Your Honour, it is actually the custom to demand the fee before the operation, as the patient is more willing to pay before an operation than after. Which is only human. In the case

157

in question I was convinced, when I started the operation, that my servant had already received the fee. In this I was mistaken.

THE INVALID: He was mistaken! A good doctor doesn't make mistakes! He examines before he operates.

AZDAK: That's right. (*To Shauwa*) Public Prosecutor, what's the other case about?

SHAUWA: (*busily sweeping*) Blackmail.

THE BLACKMAILER: High Court of Justice, I'm innocent. I only wanted to find out from the landowner concerned if he really had attacked his niece. He informed me very politely that this was not the case, and gave me the money only so I could pay for my uncle's studies.

AZDAK: Hm. (*To the Doctor*) You, on the other hand, can cite no extenuating circumstances for your offence, huh?

THE DOCTOR: Except that to err is human.

AZDAK: And you are perfectly well aware that in money matters a good doctor is conscious of his responsibility? I once heard of a doctor who made a thousand piastres out of one sprained finger: he discovered it had something to do with blood circulation, which a less good doctor might have overlooked. On another occasion he made a real gold mine out of the careful treatment of a somewhat disordered gall bladder. You have no excuse, Doctor. The corn merchant, Uxu, had his son study medicine to get some knowledge of trade, our medical schools are so good. (*To the Blackmailer*) What's the name of the landowner?

SHAUWA: He doesn't want it known.

AZDAK: In that case I will pass judgement. The court considers the blackmail proved. And you (*to the invalid*) are sentenced to a fine of one thousand piastres. If you get a second stroke, the doctor will have to treat you free. Eventually he will have to amputate. (*To the Limping Man*) As compensation you will receive a bottle of rubbing alcohol. (*To the Blackmailer*) You are sentenced to hand over half the proceeds of your deal to the Public Prosecutor to keep the landowner's name secret. You are advised, moreover, to study medicine—you seem well suited to that calling. (*To the Doctor*) You are acquitted in consideration of an unpardonable error in the practice of your profession! Next cases!

THE STORY TELLER: With a pound you're on firm ground (no one is willing for a shilling)

And the law is a cat in a sack.
But one whelp brings help to the many for a penny,
The name of this rascal?Azdak.
Azdak's judge's chair is in a tavern. Three rich farmers stand before
Azdak. Shauwa brings him wine. In a corner stands an old peasant
woman. In the open doorway, and outside, stand villagers looking
on. An Ironshirt stands guard with a banner.

AZDAK: The Public Prosecutor has the floor.

SHAUWA: It concerns a cow. For five weeks the defendant has
had a cow in her stable, the property of the farmer Suru. She was
also found to be in possession of a stolen ham, and a number of
cows belonging to Shutoff were killed after he had asked the
defendant to pay the rent on a piece of land.

THE FARMERS: It's a matter of my ham, Your Honour.

—It's a matter of my land, Your Honour.

—It's a matter of my cow, Your Honour.

AZDAK: Well, Granny, what have you got to say to all this?

THE OLD WOMAN: Your Honour, one night towards morning,
five weeks ago, there was a knock at my door, and outside stood a
bearded man with a cow, and said: 'My dear woman, I am the
miracle-working Saint Banditus and because your son has been
killed in the war, I bring you this cow as a souvenir. Take good
care of it.'

THE FARMERS: The robber, Irakli, Your Honour!

—Her brother-in-law, Your Honour!

—The cow-thief!

—The incendiary!

—He must be beheaded!

Outside, a woman screams. The crowd grows restless, retreats.
Enter the bandit Irakli with a huge axe.

THE BANDIT: A very good evening, dear friends! A glass of
vodka!

THE FARMERS: (*crossing themselves*) Irakli!

AZDAK: Public Prosecutor, a glass of vodka for our guest. And
who are you?

THE BANDIT: I'm a wandering hermit, Your Honour. And thank
you for the gracious gift. (*He empties the glass which Shauwa has*
brought.) Another!

AZDAK: I am Azdak. (*He gets up and bows. The Bandit also*

bows.) The court welcomes the foreign hermit. Go on with your story, Granny.

THE OLD WOMAN: Your Honour, that first night I didn't yet know that Saint Banditus could work miracles, it was only the cow. But one night, a few days later, the farmer's servants came to take the cow away again. Then they turned round in front of my door and went off without the cow. And on their heads sprouted bumps big as a fist. Then I knew that Saint Banditus had changed their hearts and turned them into friendly people.

(*The Bandit roars with laughter.*)

THE FIRST FARMER: I know what changed them.

AZDAK: That's fine. You can tell us later. Continue.

THE OLD WOMAN: Your Honour, the next one to become a good man was the farmer Shutoff—a devil, as everyone knows. But Saint Banditus has arranged it so that he let me off the rent on the little piece of land.

THE SECOND FARMER: Because my cows were killed in the field.

(*The Bandit laughs.*)

THE OLD WOMAN: (*answering Azdak's sign to continue*) And one morning the ham came flying in at my window. It hit me in the small of the back. I'm still lame from it, see, Your Honour. (*She limps a few steps. The Bandit laughs.*) I ask Your Honour, was there ever a time when a poor old woman could get a ham without a miracle?

(*The Bandit starts sobbing.*)

AZDAK: (*rising from his chair*) Granny, that's a question that strikes straight at the court's heart. Be so kind as to sit down here. (*Hesitating, the Old Woman sits in the Judge's chair. Azdak sits on the floor, glass in hand, reciting.*)

Granny, I almost called you Mother Grusinia the Woebegone,
The bereaved one, whose sons are at the war.
She is beaten with fists, but full of hope!
She weeps when she receives a cow
And is surprised when she is not beaten.
May you render a merciful verdict on Us the Damned!

(*Bellowing at the Farmers*) Admit that you don't believe in miracles, you atheists! Each of you is sentenced to pay five hundred piastres! For your godlessness! Get out! (*The Farmers slink out.*) And you,

Granny, and you (*to the Bandit*) pious man, empty a pitcher of wine with the Public Prosecutor and Azdak!

THE STORY TELLER: Statute and rule he broke like a loaf to feed the folk.
On the wreck of the law he brought them to the shore,
Granted their shrill demands, took bribes from the empty hands
Of the simple and the poor.

Two years and more Azdak was a wolf to the wolf pack
And weighed with a false scale.
In the judge's seat he'd stay—the gallows not far away—
The law had a sting in its tail.

THE STORY TELLER: Hear now the story of the trial
Concerning Governor Abashwili's child
And the establishing of the true mother
By the famous test of the Chalk Circle.
(*The court of justice. Ironshirts lead the child, Michael, across stage and out at the back. Ironshirts hold Grusha back with their lances under the gateway until the child has been led through. Then she is admitted. She is accompanied by the former Governor's cook. There are distant noises and a fire-red sky.*)

(*Enter the Governor's wife, followed by the Adjutant and two lawyers.*)
THE GOVERNOR'S WIFE: At least there are no *common* people here, thank God. I can't stand their smell. It always gives me migraine.
THE FIRST LAWYER: Madam, I must ask you to be as careful as possible in everything you say until we have another judge.
THE GOVERNOR'S WIFE: But I didn't say anything at all, Illo Shuboladze. I *love* the people with their simple straightforward minds! It's only their smell that brings on my migraine.
THE SECOND LAWYER: There won't be many spectators. The population is sitting at home behind locked doors because of the riots in the suburbs.
THE GOVERNOR'S WIFE: (*looking at Grusha*) Is that the creature?

THE FIRST LAWYER: Please, most gracious Natella Abashwili, I must ask you to abstain from all invective, until it is absolutely certain that the Grand Duke has appointed a new judge, and we've got rid of the present one who is about the lowest ever seen in a judge's gown. And things seem all set to move, you see.

(*Enter Ironshirts from the courtyard.*)

THE COOK: (*to Grusha*) Her Grace would pull your hair out on the spot if she didn't know Azdak is for the poor people. He goes by the face.

(*Ironshirts begin fastening a rope to a beam. Azdak, in chains, is led in, followed by Shauwa, also in chains. The three farmers bring up the rear.*)

AN IRONSHIRT: You are trying to run away, it seems. (*He strikes Azdak.*)

ONE FARMER: Off with the judge's gown before we string him up.

(*Ironshirts and farmers tear off Azdak's gown. His torn under-wear is visible. Then someone kicks him.*)

AN IRONSHIRT: (*pushing him into someone else*) If you want a heap of justice, here it is!

(*Accompanied by shouts of* 'You'll get it!' *and* 'Let me have him, brother!' *they throw Azdak back and forth until he collapses. Then he is lifted up and dragged under the noose.*)

THE GOVERNOR'S WIFE: (*who, during this 'ball-game', has clapped her hands hysterically*) I disliked that man from the moment I first saw him.

AZDAK: (*covered with blood, panting*) I can't see. Give me a rag.

AN IRONSHIRT: What is it you want to see?

AZDAK: You dogs! (*He wipes the blood out of his eyes with his shirt.*) Good morning, dogs! How goes it, dogs! How's the dog world? Does it smell good? Have you another boot to lick? Are you back at each other's throats, dogs?

(*Accompanied by a corporal, a dust-covered rider enters. He takes some documents from a leather case, looks at them, then interrupts.*)

THE RIDER: Stop! I bring a despatch from the Grand Duke, containing the latest appointments.

THE CORPORAL: (*bellowing*) Atten—shun!

THE RIDER: Of the new judge it says: 'We appoint a man whom we have to thank for the saving of a life indispensable to the country's welfare—a certain Azdak of Nuka.' Which is he?

SHAUWA: (*pointing*) That's him, Your Excellency.

THE CORPORAL: (*bellowing*) What's going on here?

AN IRONSHIRT: I ask to be allowed to report that His Honour Adzak was already His Honour Azdak, but on these farmers' denunciation was pronounced the Grand Duke's enemy.

THE CORPORAL: (*pointing at the farmers*) March them off! (*They are marched off. They bow all the time.*) See to it that His Honour Azdak is exposed to no more violence. (*Exeunt Rider and Corporal.*)

THE COOK: (*to Shauwa*) She clapped her hands! I hope he saw it!

THE FIRST LAWYER: It's a catastrophe.

(*Azdak has fainted. Coming to, he is dressed again in judge's robes. He walks, swaying, towards the Ironshirts.*)

AN IRONSHIRT: What does Your Honour desire?

AZDAK: Nothing, fellow dogs. An occasional boot to lick. (*To Shauwa*) I pardon you. (*He is unchained.*) Get me some red wine, the sweet kind. (*Shauwa stumbles off.*) Get out of here, I've got to judge a case. (*Exeunt Ironshirts. Shauwa returns with a pitcher of wine. Azdak gulps it down.*) I accept . . .

(*The prosecutors, among whom a worried council has been held, smile with relief. They whisper.*)

THE COOK: Oh dear!

SIMON: A well can't be filled with dew! they say.

THE LAWYERS: (*approaching Azdak, who stands up, expectantly*) A quite ridiculous case, Your Honour. The accused has abducted a child and refuses to hand it over.

AZDAK: (*stretching out his hand, glancing at Grusha*) A most attractive person. (*He fingers the money, then sits down, satisfied.*) I open the proceedings and demand the absolute truth. (*To Grusha*) Especially from you.

THE FIRST LAWYER: High Court of Justice! Blood, as the popular saying goes, is thicker than water. This old adage . . .

AZDAK: (*interrupting*) The Court wants to know the lawyers' fee.

THE FIRST LAWYER: (*surprised*) I beg your pardon? (*Azdak, smiling, rubs his thumb and index finger.*) Oh, I see. Five hundred piastres, Your Honour, to answer the Court's somewhat unusual question.

AZDAK: Did you hear? The question is unusual. I ask it because I listen to you in quite a different way when I know you are good.

THE FIRST LAWYER: (*bowing*) Thank you, Your Honour. High Court of Justice, of all ties the ties of blood are strongest. Mother and child—is there a more intimate relationship? Can one tear a child from its mother? High Court of Justice, she has fed it with her blood. She has borne it with pain. High Court of Justice, it has been observed that even the wild tigress, robbed of her young, roams restless through the mountains, shrunk to a shadow. Nature herself . . .

AZDAK: (*interrupting, to Grusha*) What's your answer to all this and anything else the lawyer might have to say?

GRUSHA: He's mine.

AZDAK: Is that all? I hope you can prove it. In any case I advise you to tell me why you think I should assign the child to you.

GRUSHA: I brought him up like the priest says 'according to my best knowledge and conscience'. I always found him something to eat. Most of the time he had a roof over his head. And I went to such trouble for him. I had expenses too. I didn't look out for my own comfort. I brought the child up to be friendly with everyone, and from the beginning taught him to work as well as he could. He's still a very little thing.

THE FIRST LAWYER: Your Honour, it is significant that the girl herself doesn't claim any tie of blood between her and the child.

AZDAK: The Court takes note.

THE FIRST LAWYER: Thank you, Your Honour. Please permit a woman bowed in sorrow—who has already lost her husband and now has also to fear the loss of her child—to address a few words to you. The gracious Natella Abashwili is . . .

THE GOVERNOR'S WIFE: (*quietly*) A most cruel fate, Sir, forces me to ask you to return my beloved child. It is not for me to describe to you the tortures of a bereaved mother's soul, the anxiety, the sleepless nights, the . . .

THE SECOND LAWYER: (*bursting out*) It's outrageous the way this woman is being treated. She is not allowed to enter her husband's palace. The revenue of her estates is blocked. She is cold-bloodedly told that it's tied to the heirs. She can't do anything without the child. She can't even pay her lawyers! (*To the First Lawyer who, desperate about this outburst, makes frantic gestures to keep him from speaking*) Dear Illo Shuboladze, why shouldn't it be divulged now that it's the Abashwili estates that are at stake?

THE FIRST LAWYER: Please, Honoured Sandro Oboladze! We had agreed ... (*To Azdak*) Of course it is correct that the trial will also decide whether our noble client will obtain the right to dispose of the extensive Abashwili estates. I say 'also' advisedly, for in the foreground stands the human tragedy of a mother, as Natella Abashwili rightly explained in the first words of her moving statement. Even if Michael Abashwili were *not* the heir of the estates, he would still be the dearly beloved child of my client.

AZDAK: Stop! The Court is touched by the mention of the estates. It's proof of human feeling.

THE SECOND LAWYER: Thanks, Your Honour. Dear Illo Shuboladze, we can prove in any case that the woman who took possession of the child is not the child's mother. Permit me to lay before the Court the bare facts. High Court of Justice, by an unfortunate chain of circumstances, the child Michael Abashwili was left behind while its mother was making her escape. Grusha, a palace kitchen maid, was present on that Easter Sunday and was observed to be busy with the child and ...

THE COOK: All her mistress was thinking about was what kind of dresses she'd take along!

THE SECOND LAWYER: (*unmoved*) Nearly a year later Grusha turned up in a mountain village with a child, and there entered into a state of matrimony with ...

AZDAK: How did you get into that mountain village?

GRUSHA: On foot, Your Honour. And he was mine.

SIMON: I am the father, Your Honour.

THE COOK: He was in my care, Your Honour, for five piastres.

THE SECOND LAWYER: This man is engaged to Grusha, High Court of Justice, and therefore his testimony is not trustworthy.

AZDAK: Well, I'll make it short now, and not listen to any more lies. (*To Grusha*) Especially not yours. (*To all the accused*) I can imagine what you've cooked up to cheat me! I know you! You're swindlers.

GRUSHA: (*suddenly*) I can quite understand your wanting to cut it short, now I've seen what you accepted!

AZDAK: Shut up! Did I accept anything from you?

GRUSHA: (*while the Cook tries to restrain her*) I haven't got anything.

AZDAK: That's true. Quite true. From starvelings I never get a thing. I might just as well starve, myself. You want justice, but do you want to pay for it? When you go to the butcher you know you have to pay, but you go to the judge as if you were going to a funeral supper.

SIMON: (*loudly*) When the horse was shod, the horse-fly held out its leg, as the saying is.

AZDAK: (*eagerly accepting the challenge*) Better a treasure in manure than a stone in a mountain stream.

SIMON: A fine day. Let's go fishing, said the angler to the worm.

AZDAK: I'm my own master, said the servant, and cut off his foot.

SIMON: I love you as a father, said the Czar to the peasants, and had the Czarevitch's head cut off.

AZDAK: A fool's worst enemy is himself.

SIMON: However, a smell has no nose.

AZDAK: Fined ten piastres! That'll teach you what justice is.

GRUSHA: (*furiously*) A fine kind of justice! You play fast and loose with us because we don't talk as refined as that crowd with their lawyers!

AZDAK: That's so. You people are too dumb. It's only right you should get it in the neck.

GRUSHA: Because you want to pass the child on to her. And she's too refined to know how to keep it dry! You know no more about justice than I do, I can see.

AZDAK: There's something in that. I'm an ignorant man. I haven't even a decent pair of pants under my gown. See for yourself! With me, everything goes for food and drink—I was educated at a convent. Incidentally, I'll fine you ten piastres for contempt of court. And moreover you're a very silly girl to turn me against you, instead of making eyes at me to keep me in a good temper. Twenty piastres!

GRUSHA: Even if it were thirty, I would tell you what I think of your justice, you drunken onion! (*Incoherently*) How dare you talk to me like the cracked Isaiah on the church window? As if you *were* somebody? Aren't you ashamed of yourself when you see how I tremble before you? You have made yourself their servant so no one should take their houses away, and they'd stolen them!

Since when have houses belonged to bedbugs? But you're on the watch, or they couldn't drag our men into their wars! You bribe-taker! (*Azdak half gets up, starts beaming. With his little hammer he half-heartedly knocks on the table as if to get silence. As Grusha's scolding continues, he only beats time with his hammer.*) I've no respect for you. No more than for a thief or a robber with a knife! You can do what you want. You can take the child away from me, a hundred against one, but I'll tell you one thing: only extortioners should be chosen for a profession like yours. As a punishment! They should sit in judgement on their fellow creatures. Which is worse than to hang from gallows.

AZDAK: (*sitting down*) Now it'll be thirty! And I won't go on squabbling with you as though we were in a bar. What'd happen to my dignity as a judge? Anyway, I've lost interest in your case. Where's the couple who wanted a divorce? (*To Shauwa*) Bring 'em in. This case is adjourned for fifteen minutes.

THE FIRST LAWYER: (*to the Governor's wife*) Even without using the rest of the evidence, Madam, we have the verdict in the bag.

THE COOK: (*to Grusha*) You've gone and spoiled your chances with him. You won't get the child now.

THE GOVERNOR'S WIFE: Shalva, my smelling salts!

(*Enter a very old couple.*)

AZDAK: I accept . . . (*The Old Couple don't understand.*) I hear you want to be divorced. How long have you been living together?

THE OLD WOMAN: Forty years, Your Honour.

AZDAK: And why do you want a divorce?

THE OLD MAN: We don't like each other, Your Honour.

AZDAK: Since when?

THE OLD WOMAN: Oh, from the very beginning, Your Honour.

AZDAK: I'll think about your request and render my verdict when I'm through with the other case. (*Shauwa leads them back.*) I need the child. (*He beckons Grusha to him, and bends not unkindly toward her.*) I've noticed you have a soft spot for justice. I don't believe he's your child, but if he were yours, woman, wouldn't you want him to be rich? You'd only have to say he isn't yours. And immediately he'd have a palace and many horses in his stable and many beggars on his doorstep and many soldiers in his service and many petitioners in his courtyard, wouldn't he? What do you say—don't you want him to be rich?

(*Grusha is silent.*)

THE STORY TELLER: Hear now what the angry girl thought but did not say:

'If he went in golden shoes
He would cruel be
Evil then would be his life.
He could laugh at me.

'Too heavy is a heart of stone
For human breast to bear!
Bad and powerful to be
Is too great a care.

'Hunger he will have to fear
But no hungry one!
Darkness he will have to fear
But not the sun!'

AZDAK: I think I understand you, woman.

GRUSHA: (*suddenly*) I won't give him up. I've raised him and he knows me.

(*Enter Shauwa with the child.*)

THE GOVERNOR'S WIFE: It's in rags!

GRUSHA: That's not true. I wasn't given time to put his good shirt on.

THE GOVERNOR'S WIFE: It must have been in a pigsty.

GRUSHA: (*furiously*) I'm not a pig, but there are others who are. Where did you leave your child?

THE GOVERNOR'S WIFE: I'll show you, you vulgar creature! (*She is about to throw herself on Grusha, but is restrained by her Lawyers.*) She's a criminal, she must be whipped. Immediately!

THE SECOND LAWYER: (*holding his hand over her mouth*) Gracious Natella Abashwili, you promised . . . Your Honour, the plaintiff's nerves . . .

AZDAK: Plaintiff and defendant! The Court has listened to your case, and has come to no decision as to who the real mother of this child is. I, as a judge, am obliged to choose a mother for the child. I'll make a test. Shauwa, get a piece of chalk and draw a circle on the floor. (*Shauwa does so.*) Now place the child in the centre. (*Shauwa puts Michael, who smiles at Grusha, in the centre of the circle*.) Stand next the circle, both of you. (*The Governor's Wife and Grusha step up to the circle*.) Now each of you take the child by one hand. (*They do so*.) The true mother is she who has the strength to pull the child out of the circle toward herself.

THE SECOND LAWYER: (*quickly*) High Court of Justice, I object! The fate of the great Abashwili estates, which are bound to the child, as the heir, should not be made dependent on such a doubtful duel. In addition, my client does not command the strength of this person, wo is accustomed to physical work.

AZDAK: She looks pretty well fed to me. Pull! (*The Governor's Wife pulls the child out of the circle on her side. Grusha lets go and stands aghast*.) What's the matter with you? You didn't pull!

GRUSHA: I didn't hold on to him.

THE FIRST LAWYER: (*congratulating the Governor's Wife*) What did I say! The ties of blood!

GRUSHA: (*running to Azdak*) Your Honour, I take back everything I said against you. I ask your forgiveness. If only I could keep him till he can speak all the words. He knows a few.

AZDAK: Don't influence the Court. I bet you only know twenty yourself. All right, I'll do the test once more, to make certain. (*The two women take up their positions again*.) Pull! (*Again Grusha lets go of the child*.)

GRUSHA: (*in despair*) I brought him up! Am I to tear him to pieces? I can't do it!

AZDAK: (*rising*) And in this manner the Court has established the true mother. (*To Grusha*) Take your child and be off. I advise you not to stay in the city with him. (*To the Governor's Wife*) And you disappear before I fine you for fraud. Your estates fall to the city. They'll be converted into a playground for children. They need one, and I've decided it shall be called after me; Azdak's Garden. (*The Governor's Wife has fainted and is carried out by the Lawyers and the Adjutant. Grusha stands motionless. Shauwa leads the child toward her*.) Now I'll take off this judge's gown—it has grown too hot for me. I'm not cut out for a hero. In token of farewell, I invite you all to a little dance outside on the meadow.

THE STORY TELLER: And after that evening Azdak disappeared and was not seen again.
The people of Grusinia did not forget him but long remembered

The period of his judging as a brief golden age
Almost an age of justice.
(*All the couples dance off. Azdak has disappeared.*)
But you, you who have listened to the Story of the Chalk Circle,
Take note what men of old concluded:
That what there is shall go to those who are good for it,
Thus: the children to the motherly, that they prosper
The carts to the good drivers, that they are well driven
And the valley to the waterers, that it bring forth fruit.

The Bitter Comedy of France

RING ROUND THE MOON

(An excerpt from Act III, Scene I)

by

Jean Anouilh

(Translated by Christopher Fry)

CHARACTERS

ISABELLE, *a ballet dancer.*
MESSERSCHMANN, *a melancholy millionaire.*
JOSHUA, *a crumbling butler.*

THE AUTHOR

Jean Anouilh was born in Bordeaux in 1910, but came to Paris when he was young for his education. He spent some time at the Law Faculty in Paris, then two years in an advertising firm, but he was more interested in writing. After the production of his first play he decided to live entirely by writing for plays and films. He has written a great deal, including twenty-five plays, and he still continues. He has been one of France's best known and best loved playwrights for many years. His plays vary from light and witty comedies to the more sombre type of drama known as 'black' comedies. Some of his plays are *Time Remembered*, *Point of Departure*, *Antigone*, *Ring Round the Moon*, *Waltz of the Toreadors* and *Beckett*.

THE PLAY

L'Invitation au Château was translated by Christopher Fry as *Ring Round the Moon* and is one of Anouilh's most popular plays. It is a highly mannered piece of theatrical nonsense, but its wit and charm and it's underlying note of satire and criticism of social values makes it more than a gay trifle. Indeed even the most apparently frivolous of Anouilh's plays have this other mood, a sad awareness of the folly of man's pretensions, of his illusions about love, of his desperate reliance on material things like money and position. In this play, a young aristocratic man, Hugo, is in love with a rich girl called Diana, who because she is annoyed with him has become engaged to his twin brother, Frederic. Hugo decides to make her jealous by inviting to the engagement ball at the château, a beautiful young dancer called Isabelle. She is hired to play this part, but although she is poor she has plenty of spirit, and after she has been attacked by Diana she tells everyone what she thinks of the petty conspiracy. Frederic finds she is a real person and begins to fall in love with her. Diana's millionaire father, Messerschmann, tries to get rid of her by offering her a fortune if she will leave, but she refuses. The scene we have included is this one. The remainder of the play traces the various complications that ensue before Diana turns to Hugo, and Isabelle and Frederic are free to marry. The plot is in outline a romantic and conventional one, but the scene included shows that the treatment is far from conventional.

RING ROUND THE MOON

Act III, Scene I

The scene is a rococo winter garden; glass and wrought-iron;
yellow plush curtains and green plants. It looks out on to a wide
expanse of park.
Isabelle and Messerschmann are talking together.

MESSER: (*speaking straight out*) Now, young lady, I'm going to
be rather brutal. I know who you are, and in half an hour's time
everybody will know. The party's over, as far as you're concerned.
You've had a great success, everybody's been charmed by you,
but it was a little adventure which couldn't last. I've come to ask
you to cut it even shorter. Go up to your room and disappear
without seeing anyone again. And I shall be most grateful to you.

ISABELLE: How can it affect you whether I go or stay?

MESSER: It's a little present I should like to give my daughter.
You see, I make no bones about it. I've never deceived anyone in
my business affairs, and I've always succeeded. How much do you
want?

ISABELLE: Nothing. I had decided to go before you asked me.

MESSER: I know. But it isn't fair that you should go without
being paid. How much did Hugo promise you?

ISABELLE: My usual dancing fee, and this dress, which someone
has torn.

MESSER: Who tore it?

ISABELLE: Your daughter.

MESSER: Then that's my business too. As well as what you were
going to ask me, I'll pay for two more dresses.

ISABELLE: Thank you, but I'm happy with this one, with the
tear.

MESSER: Let's get the situation clear. I don't want you to
see Hugo again, even to get your fee. How much do I pay you
to go without seeing him?

ISABELLE: Nothing at all. I didn't expect to see him.

MESSER: But how about the money he promised you?

ISABELLE: I don't intend to take it. I can be said to have danced here this evening for my own pleasure.

(*Messerschmann looks at her for a moment, in silence, then weightily and powerfully moves towards her.*)

MESSER: I don't like it when things don't cost anything, young lady.

ISABELLE: Does it disturb you?

MESSER: It's too expensive. Why are you refusing Hugo's money?

ISABELLE: Because I'm glad not to take it.

MESSER: And mine?

ISABELLE: Because you haven't any reason to give it to me. I was asked to act in a comedy here this evening. My performance is over, the curtain is down, and I'm going home.

MESSER: But not with nothing to show for it?

ISABELLE: Why not?

MESSER: It's not as it should be.

ISABELLE: I'm sorry, but it's what I'm going to do. You will excuse me. (*She starts to go.*)

MESSER: (*suddenly furious*) No, no, no! Don't be like Ossowitch!

ISABELLE: (*stops, astonished*) Like Ossowitch?

MESSER: Yes. He was a banker of a rival group, and I had to have important discussions with him. I never met such a man for getting up and going. Whenever we disagreed, which was pretty often, he got up and went. Every time I had to catch up with him in the vestibule or in the lift or somewhere. And the farther I had to go to catch him, the more it cost me. In the end I had to invite him to come out in a canoe, when I'd first made quite sure he couldn't swim. After that we were wonderfully good friends: but now he has learnt to swim and things are not so nice. So don't you start this getting up and going, my dear child, it isn't a good way to talk. Nobody ever agrees with anybody in a business discussion, but we stay sitting, or else business is no good. Now, come along, my dear young lady, be reasonable. Strike a good bargain with me before it's too late. What do you want?

ISABELLE: Nothing.

MESSER: It's too much. Now, look, I'm going to be foolish. I'm going to offer you twice what you expect. I've the notes on me here. (*He brings a bundle of notes from his pocket.*) Look at this bundle here, such virgins and so clean, such a pretty little bunch!

It would be very nice, you will agree with me, to carry about a sprig or two or these little papers?

ISABELLE: How should I carry them?

MESSER: (*suddenly like a shopkeeper*) Would you like me to wrap them up for you? I could make a nice little parcel of them.

ISABELLE: Listen. I don't want to have to walk out like Mr. Ossowitch; I don't want to bring back unhappy memories to you; but I insist that you believe me. I don't want your money.

MESSER: (*pocketing the notes, furious*) You're being very exorbitant.

ISABELLE: (*looks at him and says*) Is it really possible to be a great power in the world without being very intelligent?

MESSER: I am intelligent! I'm very intelligent! It's because I'm very intelligent and experienced that I tell you I don't believe you!

ISABELLE: (*taking him gently by the arm*) Then, if you're intelligent, let's talk intelligently. If you hadn't kept me here I should have been gone already. So you see I have nothing to sell.

MESSER: (*angrily*) There's always something to sell! Anyway, even if you haven't, I've got to buy something now we've started bargaining.

ISABELLE: Why?

MESSER: Why? Because I should lose all faith in myself if I didn't.

ISABELLE: (*with a slight smile*) If it takes so little to make you lose faith, I must write to Mr. Ossowitch.

MESSER: (*calmer*) Ossowitch was a baby. But you're an opponent who interests me. What I'm buying from you now isn't my daughter's peace of mind any more, it's my own peace of mind. And I put no limit whatsoever on that. How much do you want?

ISABELLE: Do men become masters of the world by continually repeating themselves?

MESSER: You're as rich as any girl in the house tonight. And if I want it, Romainville shall adopt you: you really will be his niece!

ISABELLE: Thank you.

MESSER: Listen. I'll make you so rich, the grandest and handsomest young fellow here will ask you to marry him immediately.

ISABELLE: I'm sorry. But none of that will please me as much as saying No to you.

MESSER: (*suddenly howling*) Whatever shall I do? I don't believe in money any more either! All it gives me is dust, smoke, nausea, and indigestion. I eat noodles and I drink water, and I get no pleasure at all from my frozen snow-queen mistress: I don't even suffer when she deceives me, because I don't really want her: I want nothing at all! I'm a poor little tailor from Cracow, and my only really pleasant memory is the first suit I made when I was sixteen: a jacket for a priest, and it turned out very well. My father said to me: 'This time you have done it well: you know now what your calling is.' And I was happy . . . but since then I've succeeded at nothing, except at making money, more and more money, and money has never made anybody love me, not even my own daughter. Please be sympathetic. Do stand by me this evening. Take my money!

ISABELLE: No.

MESSER: No? Ah well: now you can see what I'll do with these beautiful little bundles which can't do anything: I'll bite them and tear them with my teeth and spit them on the ground!

(*He has taken the bundle of notes and starts tearing them with his own teeth; then, soon, for the sake of speed, with his hands.*)

ISABELLE: (*joyfully*) What a good idea! Give me some, I'll help you. This will make me feel much better!

(*She takes some of the bundles and starts happily and quietly tearing them up. They throw the scraps of paper into the air. They both work feverishly in a rain of paper.*)

MESSER: (*in a kind of fury*) There! So! So! There! That's a country house: the dream of all the small householders!

ISABELLE: (*tearing away merrily*) With the garden, the pond, the goldfish, the roses!

MESSER: Everything! There goes a business. A millinery business: the one I was going to give you, like the fool I was!

ISABELLE: (*tearing*) Hooray! That was a hat!

MESSER: (*annoyed, but not stopping*) Why only one hat?

ISABELLE: It was very expensive!

MESSER: There go the dresses, and still more dresses, rolls and folds and billows of material, what they're all dying to put on their backs. There go the cloaks and the coats and the wraps and the furs!

ISABELLE: (*tearing*) Not too many: it's nearly summer-time!

MESSER: Away goes the beautiful linen, the satin sheets, petticoats as light as cobwebs, embroidered handkerchiefs!

ISABELLE: (*tearing*) There goes a trunk!

MESSER: (*stopping in surprise*) Why a trunk?

ISABELLE: To put everything into!

MESSER: (*starting again*) There go the necklaces, the bracelets, the rings—all the rings!

ISABELLE: (*tearing*) Oh! Such a beautiful pearl!

MESSER: You'll regret that!

ISABELLE: (*taking more to tear*) No, not a bit!

MESSER: Away go the holidays abroad, the servants, the racehorses, the beautiful ladies ready and willing, away go the consciences of honest men, and all the prosperity of this lamentable world! There! There! There! There! (*He tears the last of the notes and turns to her.*) Are you happy now?

ISABELLE: (*softly*) No. Are you?

MESSER: Not at all.

(*They are kneeling side by side, exhausted. Isabelle finds one untorn note on the ground and tears it up.*)

ISABELLE: There go the poor! We'd forgotten them. (*A pause. She looks at the exhausted Messerschmann and asks him gently*) I bet it wasn't so exhausting to get it all?

MESSER: I'm very unhappy.

ISABELLE: (*with a wry smile*) Me, too.

MESSER: I understand very well how you feel. And I'm the only person in this house this evening who does understand. For a long time, such a long time, I was humiliated, until I became stronger than they were. Then I could turn the tables. Every man is quite alone. That's definite. No one can help anyone else: he can only go on.

(*They both look straight in front of them, squatting on the ground in the middle of the torn notes. Joshua enters and finds them so, to his surprise.*)

MESSER: (*seeing him*) What do you want?

JOSHUA: It's Mr. Hugo, sir: he wishes to speak to the young lady in the little drawing-room, to settle her account.

ISABELLE: (*getting up*) Tell him he doesn't owe me anything. Mr. Messerschmann has paid me.

(*She goes. Messerschmann watches her go, then rises with difficulty, with Joshua's help.*)

MESSER: My friend.

JOSHUA: Sir?

MESSER: You seem to have a pleasant face.

JOSHUA: (*after the first astonishment*) I belong to a generation of old servants who could never permit themselves to have such a thing while on duty, sir. But on Sundays, and particularly on holidays, my friends tell me I have an amiable face, sir, almost jovial, what I hope I may call a nice face, very French and homely, sir.

MESSER: Then listen to me. You must have read your Bible when you were a little boy?

JOSHUA: Here and there, sir, like everybody else.

MESSER: Did you ever come across Samson?

JOSHUA: The gentleman who had his hair cut, sir?

MESSER: Yes; and he was very unhappy. Jeered at, my friend, always jeered at by everybody. They had put his eyes out. They thought he was blind, but I'm sure he could see.

JOSHUA: Quite possible, sir . . .

MESSER: And then, one fine day, unable to stand it any more, he got them to lead him between the pillars of the temple. He was very strong, terribly strong, you understand? He twined his arms round the pillars . . . (*He puts his arms round the dismayed Joshua.*) Like this!

JOSHUA: Oh, sir! Do take care, sir, someone will see us!

MESSER: And then he shook them with all his might. (*He shakes Joshua.*)

JOSHUA: (*being shaken*) Yes, sir! Do be careful, sir! I'm the one who will get into trouble!

MESSER: (*letting him go with a sigh, his feelings relieved*) There!

JOSHUA: (*putting himself to rights*) Well, there, sir. (*He adds, for something to say*) It wasn't at all the thing to do in church . . .

MESSER: (*with a dark chuckle*) You might well say so. He was so strong the entire temple crumbled down on to the two thousand Philistines who were there praying to their false gods, and thinking Samson no better than a fool!

JOSHUA: But it fell on him, too, sir.

MESSER: It fell on him, too. But that wasn't of any importance. How could being poor hurt him!

JOSHUA: If you say so, sir.

(*A pause. Joshua starts to go.*)

MESSER: My friend.

JOSHUA: Sir?

MESSER: I'm putting through an overseas telephone call from my room tonight.

JOSHUA: Certainly, sir.

MESSER: That's all. Like Samson. With my eyes tight shut.

JOSHUA: (*going*) Quite so, sir.

MESSER: And all at once there's a frightful uproar, a telephone ringing in the small hours. And that is the temple starting to crumble. Do you understand?

JOSHUA: No, sir.

MESSER: It doesn't matter. (*He finds a forgotten note in his pocket and gives it to Joshua.*) Here's a thousand francs. Forget everything I've said. (*As he goes out, he turns and says*) And for supper, you remember . . . without butter.

JOSHUA: (*bowing*) And without salt.

The Theatre of the Absurd

MAID TO MARRY

A One Act Play

by

Eugene Ionesco

(Translated by Donald Watson)

CHARACTERS

GENTLEMAN.
LADY.
GENTLEMAID.

THE AUTHOR

Eugene Ionesco was born in Roumania in 1912 but spent his early years in Paris so that French was his first language, and became the language in which he wrote. Though he returned to Roumania at various times, and saw much of the trouble and upsets in that country, he made France his home and now lives in Paris. He became interested in the theatre when his first short play *The Bald Prima Donna* was produced in Paris, and he has gone on writing strange and sometimes difficult plays as the centre of the 'theatre of the absurd'. Some of his plays are *The Chairs*, *The Lesson*, *The Killer* and *Rhinoceros*, and these in translation have been played in England, America and Australia.

THE PLAY

Maid to Marry (*La Jeune Fille à Marier*) was first performed in 1953. It is a short one-act play, and is an example of 'theatre of the absurd' in its lighter form. All such plays are in essence satires on the ideas and customs of society. It was common in such plays to satirize the conversation of people as being conducted in clichès, and saying really nothing. In this play a lady and a gentleman carry on a serious conversation completely composed of clichès. It is meant to be played 'straight' and quite seriously and then becomes very funny. There is another comic element, that of surprise. The lady discusses her young and innocent daughter who has just completed her studies. The daughter appears at the end. 'She is a man, about thirty years old, robust and virile, with a bushy black moustache, wearing a grey suit.' The play ends with this shock of surprise. Is the lady deluded? Ionesco is having fun in showing, by absurd means, that often a person's conception of another person is very far from the truth, may indeed be a complete illusion. Some parents indeed have no knowledge of the sort of people their children really are.

MAID TO MARRY

The lady is wearing a flowered hat with a big hatpin, a long dress and a short tight-fitting purple jacket. She is carrying a handbag. The gentleman has a frock coat, a high stiff collar and stiff cuffs, a black cravat and a white beard.

They are sitting on a bench in a public park.

LADY: My daughter, let me tell you, was quite brilliant in her studies.

GENTLEMAN: I didn't know, but I'm not surprised. I knew she had plenty of pluck.

LADY: *I've* had no cause to complain, like so many parents. She's always given us perfect satisfaction.

GENTLEMAN: The credit is all yours. You brought her up properly. The model child is very rare, especially nowadays.

LADY: How right you are! . . .

GENTLEMAN: In my time children were far more obedient, more attached to their parents. They understood the sacrifices they make, their material problems and their difficulties . . . though from some points of view it's better for them not to.

LADY: I agree! . . . They were also far more . . .

GENTLEMAN: They were far more numerous.

LADY: Indeed they were. It seems the birth-rate's falling in France.

GENTLEMAN: It has its ups and downs. Just now it rather shows a tendency to rise again. But we can hardly make up for the lean years! . . .

LADY: I should say not indeed, you're certainly right there! Just imagine!

GENTLEMAN: What can you expect? It's not easy to bring children up at the present time! . . .

LADY: Indeed it's not! You don't have to tell *me* that! It's costing more and more to keep alive! And think of all the things they need! What is there they *don't* want?

GENTLEMAN: What's it all leading to? . . . Today human life is the only thing that's cheap!

LADY: Oh . . . I *do* so agree with that! . . . Now that's *very* true . . . You're *perfectly* right there . . .

GENTLEMAN: There are earthquakes, accidents, cars and all sorts of other vehicles like aeroplanes, social sickness, voluntary suicide, the atom bomb . . .

LADY: Oh, *that thing*! . . . It appears it's changed the weather for us! We don't know where we are with our seasons now, it's upset everything! . . . And if only that was all . . . but look, listen, do you know what I've heard people say? . . .

GENTLEMAN: Oh! . . . They say so many things! If you had to believe everything you hear!

LADY: That's true of course . . . There'd be no end to it, indeed there wouldn't! . . . The papers too, there's a pack of lies for you, lies, all lies! . . .

GENTLEMAN: Do as I do, Madame, trust nobody, believe in nothing, don't let them stuff your brain with rubbish! . . .

LADY: I agree. You're better off without. Indeed you are. You've got *your* head screwed on all right. You really have.

GENTLEMAN: Oh, I just *use* mine, that's all!

LADY: You're right there! . . . But you can't say the same of everyone . . .

GENTLEMAN: Nowadays you see, Madame, with all our amusements, entertainment and excitement, the cinema, income tax, gramophone record libraries, telephone, radio, air travel, big department stores . . .

LADY: Ah yes, now you've *said* it!

GENTLEMAN: The prisons, the Grands Boulevards, Social Security, and all that . . .

LADY: How right you are . . .

GENTLEMAN: All these things that make the charm of modern life have changed men and women, changed them to such a point that they're unrecognizable! . . .

LADY: Not changed them for the better either, *now* you've said it.

GENTLEMAN: And yet we can't deny progress, when we see it progressing every day . . .

LADY: How right you are . . .

GENTLEMAN: . . . in technology, applied science, mechanics, literature and art . . .

LADY: Of course. We must be fair. It isn't nice to be *un*fair.

GENTLEMAN: You could even go so far as to say that civilization's constantly developing, and in the right direction, thanks to the united efforts of all nations . . .

LADY: Perfectly true. I was just about to say the same thing.

GENTLEMAN: We've come a long way since the days of our ancestors, who used to live in caves and gobble each other up and feed on sheepskins! . . . What a long way we've come!

LADY: Yes, we have, haven't we? . . . And central heating, Monsieur, what about central heating? Did they have that in their caves?

GENTLEMAN: Well now, dear lady, when I was a small child . . .

LADY: Such a pretty age!

GENTLEMAN: . . . I used to live in the country. I remember it was still the sun that kept us warm, winter and summer alike. We used to light our homes with oil—it's true it wasn't so dear in those days—and sometimes even with candles! . . .

LADY: That happens even today, when the electricity fails.

GENTLEMAN: Machines are not perfect either. They are invented by man and they've all *his* faults!

LADY: Don't talk to me about the faults of men! Oh la la! I know all about that, they're no better than the women, they're all alike, nothing to choose between them.

GENTLEMAN: Of course. So why expect a man to do a job even a machine can't do . . .

LADY: I admit I'd never thought of that . . . yes, when you really come to think about it, it's possible after all, why not? . . .

GENTLEMAN: You see, Madame, mankind's future's in the future. It's just the opposite for animals and plants . . . But we mustn't think of the machine as a *Deus ex machina* who'll take the place of God and progress without the slightest effort on our part. On the contrary, Madame . . .

LADY: I never said we should!

GENTLEMAN: On the contrary, I say, man is still the best human machine! It's man who controls the machine . . . because he's the mind.

LADY: Now *you've* said it.

GENTLEMAN: . . . and a machine's just a machine, except for the calculating machine, which calculates by itself . . .

LADY: That's very true, it calculates by itself, what you say is perfectly correct . . .

GENTLEMAN: It's just the exception that proves the rule . . .
Look here, just now we were talking about oil and candles. In
those days an egg cost a sou and not a sou more! . . .

LADY: Impossible!

GENTLEMAN: Believe it or not! . . .

LADY: It's not that I doubt your word!

GENTLEMAN: You could dine for twenty sous, food cost nothing
then . . .

LADY: It's a different story now!

GENTLEMAN: . . . You could have a good pair of shoes, good
leather too, for three francs seventy-five centimes . . . Young folk
today don't know what that means!

LADY: They don't know when they're well-off! The young
are so ungrateful!

GENTLEMAN: Nowadays everything's a thousand times dearer.
So how can we really maintain that the machine's a happy invention
and progress a good thing?

LADY: We can't, of course!

GENTLEMAN: You'll probably say that progress can be good
or bad, like Jews or Germans or films! . . .

LADY: Oh no, I wouldn't say a thing like that!

GENTLEMAN: Why not? You could if you liked, you've a right
to, haven't you?

LADY: Of course I have! . . .

GENTLEMAN: I respect everyone's right to an opinion. My
ideas are up to date. After all, there has been a French Revolution,
and the Crusades, and the Inquisition, and Kaiser William, the
Popes, the Renaissance, Louis XIV and all that trouble for
nothing! . . . We've paid dearly enough for the right to say whatever
comes into our heads, without having people make fun of us . . .

LADY: We certainly have! . . . This land's our home! . . . We
won't have anyone come and upset us in our own place . . .

GENTLEMAN: And Joan of Arc? Have you ever wondered what
she would say, if she could see all this?

LADY: That's a question I've asked myself more than once!

GENTLEMAN: Radio! . . . And *she* used to live in an old cottage!
With all these modern transformations, she wouldn't know it any
more!

LADY: Oh no, she certainly wouldn't know it if she saw it now!

GENTLEMAN: And yet, perhaps she would after all!

LADY: Yes, you're right, perhaps she would after all!

GENTLEMAN: To think she was burnt alive by those Englishmen and then they became our allies . . .

LADY: Who'd ever have thought it?

GENTLEMAN: There are *some* good Englishmen too . . .

LADY: But they're mostly bad!

GENTLEMAN: You needn't think the Corsicans are any better!

LADY: That's not what I meant! . . .

GENTLEMAN: At least they serve one good purpose. All French postmen are Corsican. Who'd bring us our mail if there weren't any postmen!

LADY: They're a necessary evil.

GENTLEMAN: Evil is never necessary.

LADY: How right you are, that's very true!

GENTLEMAN: Don't think I look down on a postman's profession.

LADY: Every profession has its points.

GENTLEMAN: (*rising to his feet*) Madame, that is a profound observation! It deserves to pass into the language as a proverb. Allow me to congratulate you . . . (*He kisses her hand.*) Here is the *Croix d'honneur.* (*He pins a medal on the Lady's bosom.*)

LADY: (*embarrassed*) Oh, Monsieur! . . . After all, I'm only a woman! . . . But if you really mean it!

GENTLEMAN: I promise you I do, Madame. The Truth may spring from any brain . . .

LADY: Flatterer!

GENTLEMAN: (*sitting down again*) Madame, you've laid your finger on the principal vice of our society, which I detest and condemn in its entirety, without wishing to cut myself off from it . . .

LADY: You must never do that.

GENTLEMAN: Our society, Madame, no longer respects a profession. You've only to see how the country people stream into our sprawling towns . . .

LADY: Yes, Monsieur, I see.

GENTLEMAN: When there's no respect for a profession, there's none for a child, and the child, if you don't find I express myself too strongly, is the father of the man.

LADY: Quite true.

GENTLEMAN: Perhaps too the child has forgotten how to win respect!

LADY: Perhaps.

GENTLEMAN: And yet we ought to respect a child, for if there weren't any children, the human race would very soon die out.

LADY: That's what I was thinking! . . .

GENTLEMAN: Loss of respect for one thing leads to another and in the end you don't even respect your own word, when you give it.

LADY: It's terrible!

GENTLEMAN: It's all the more serious when you think that the Word is divine, like the Word of God, we've no right to take it lightly . . .

LADY: I agree with you perfectly. That's exactly why I wanted to be sure my daughter had a sound education and a respectable profession, so she can stand on her own feet, earn an honourable living and learn to respect others by starting with herself.

GENTLEMAN: You've been very wise. What has she been doing?

LADY: She's gone a long way with her studies. I've always longed for her to be a typist. So has she. She's just got her diploma. She's going to join a firm that deals in fraudulent transactions . . .

GENTLEMAN: She must be very proud and happy.

LADY: She's dancing for joy from morning to night. She's worked so hard, poor little soul!

GENTLEMAN: Now she's won the reward for her labours.

LADY: It only remains for me now to find her a good husband.

GENTLEMAN: She's a fine girl.

LADY: (*looking out into the wings*) Well now, there *is* my daughter just coming. I'll introduce you to her.

(*The Lady's daughter comes in. She is a man, about thirty years old, robust and virile, with a bushy black moustache, wearing a grey suit.*)

GENTLEMAID: Good morning, Mummy.

(*A very strong masculine voice. The gentleman-daughter kisses the Lady.*)

GENTLEMAN: She's the spitting image of you, Madame.

LADY: (*to Gentlemaid*) Go and say good-morning to the gentle-man.

GENTLEMAID: (*curtseying first*) Good-morning, Monsieur!

GENTLEMAN: Good-morning, my dear! (*To the Lady*) She's really very well brought-up. How old is she?

LADY: Ninety-three!

GENTLEMAN: She's passed her majority then?

LADY: No. She owes us eighty years, so that makes her only thirteen.

GENTLEMAN: They'll pass, you know, as quickly as the others! (*to the Gentlemaid*) Well now, so you're a minor?

GENTLEMAID: (*in a very powerful voice*) Yes, but don't forget: Many a minor mates a major!

(*The Gentleman and the Lady rise to their feet horrified. They all look at each other petrified, the Lady with clasped hands.*)

Curtain

WAITING FOR GODOT

(An excerpt from Act I)

by

Samuel Beckett

CHARACTERS

ESTRAGON, *a tramp, waiting for Godot.*
VLADIMIR, *another tramp, doing the same.*
POZZO, *a gentleman passing by.*
LUCKY, *his slave.*
A BOY, *messenger of Godot*

THE AUTHOR

Samuel Beckett was born in Ireland in 1906 and graduated with great distinction from Trinity College, Dublin. Later, studying in Paris, he became a friend of James Joyce, another Irishman living there in exile. From then on he spent a great deal of his time in Paris, and wrote most of his works in French. He makes his own translations into English. He is considered to be one of the most important writers of the 'theatre of the absurd'. His plays include *Waiting for Godot, Endgame* and *Happy Days.*

THE PLAY

Waiting for Godot is the first, and some would say, the best of Beckett's plays. It was first produced in 1952, and has puzzled and fascinated audiences all over the world. It concerns two tramps, Vladimir and Estragon, who spend their time in seemingly futile conversation while they await the arrival of Mr. Godot. The scene is a country road with a tree; it is nowhere in particular,

an empty landscape. They are tired of waiting and bored with living. Along the road comes Pozzo, driving his slave Lucky by means of a rope around his neck. Pozzo has a whip to keep Lucky in order. Lucky is burdened with a heavy bag, a folding stool, a picnic basket and a greatcoat. Pozzo has his lunch, then makes Lucky entertain the others by dancing and thinking aloud. At the end Lucky falls, exhausted by his performance, and they have to get him on his feet again. This is the point at which the extract we have chosen begins.

There are many explanations as to what the play means. Mr. Godot never does arrive; he just sends vague messages by a boy. The play does not tell a story, it explores a situation. As Estragon says: 'Nothing happens, nobody comes, nobody goes, it's awful.' Gradually we realize that the play is not about Godot at all, it is about waiting. The two tramps fill in the time by idle games and conversation. Yet a message and a meaning emerges. This is a serious example of 'theatre of the absurd'. Beckett would hope each person would find his own meaning.

WAITING FOR GODOT

An excerpt from Act I

*The scene is a country road, in a bare landscape with one tree.
Lucky is lying on the ground where he has fallen over. Pozzo is trying
to get him to his feet. Vladimir and Estragon are watching. Pozzo
is jerking the rope around Lucky's neck.*

POZZO: Up pig!

ESTRAGON: Perhaps he's dead.

VLADIMIR: You'll kill him.

POZZO: Up scum! (*He jerks the rope. Then he turns to the others*)
Help me!

VLADIMIR: How?

POZZO: Raise him up!

(*Vladimir and Estragon hoist Lucky to his feet, support him
for an instant, then let him go. He falls.*)

ESTRAGON: He's doing it on purpose!

POZZO: You must hold him. Come on, come on, raise him up!

ESTRAGON: To hell with him!

VLADIMIR: Come on, once more.

ESTRAGON: What does he take us for?

(*They raise Lucky and hold him up.*)

POZZO: Don't let him go! (*Vladimir and Estragon totter*) Don't
move! (*Pozzo fetches the bag and basket*) Hold him tight!

(*He puts the bag in Lucky's hand. Lucky drops it immediately.*)

POZZO: Don't let him go! (*He tries again. Gradually at the feel
of the bag Lucky recovers his senses and his fingers close round the
handle.*) Hold him tight! (*As before with the basket.*) Now. You can
let him go. (*Vladimir and Estragon move away from Lucky who
totters, reels, sags, but succeeds in remaining on his feet. Pozzo steps
back and cracks his whip.*) Forward! (*Lucky takes a step forward.*)
Back! (*Lucky takes a step back.*) Turn! (*Lucky turns.*) Done it!
He can walk. (*Turning to Vladimir and Estragon.*) Thank you
gentlemen, and let me—(*he fumbles in his pockets*)—let me wish
you—(*fumbles*)—wish you—(*fumbles*)—what have I done with my
watch? (*Fumbles*) A genuine half-hunter, gentlemen, with deadbeat

escapement! (*Sobbing*) 'Twas my granpa gave it to me! (*He searches on the ground. So do the others.*) Well now isn't that—

VLADIMIR: Perhaps it's in your fob.

POZZO: Wait. (*He doubles up in an attempt to apply his ear to his stomach, listens. Silence.*) I hear nothing. (*He beckons Vladimir and Estragon to him. They bend over his stomach.*) Surely one should hear the tick-tick.

VLADIMIR: Silence! (*All listen bent double.*)

ESTRAGON: I hear something.

POZZO: Where?

VLADIMIR: It's the heart.

POZZO: (*disappointed*) Damnation!

VLADIMIR: Silence!

ESTRAGON: Perhaps it has stopped. (*They straighten up.*)

POZZO: Which of you smells so bad?

ESTRAGON: He has stinking breath and I have stinking feet.

POZZO: I must go.

ESTRAGON: And your half-hunter?

POZZO: I must have left it at the manor. (*Silence.*)

ESTRAGON: Then adieu.

POZZO: Adieu.

VLADIMIR: Adieu.

ESTRAGON: Adieu. (*Silence. No one moves.*)

VLADIMIR: Adieu.

POZZO: Adieu.

ESTRAGON: Adieu. (*Silence.*)

POZZO: And thank you.

VLADIMIR: Thank *you.*

POZZO: Not at all.

ESTRAGON: Yes, yes.

POZZO: No, no.

VLADIMIR: Yes, yes.

ESTRAGON: No, no. (*Silence.*)

POZZO: I don't seem to be able . . . (*he hesitates*) . . . to depart.

ESTRAGON: Such is life.

(*Pozzo turns, moves away from Lucky, paying out the rope as he goes.*)

VLADIMIR: You're going the wrong way.

POZZO: I need a running start. (*Having come to the end of the rope, he stops, turns and cries*) Stand back! (*Vladimir and Estragon stand back. Pozzo cracks the whip*) On! On!

ESTRAGON: On! On!

VLADIMIR: On! On! (*Crack of whip. Lucky moves off.*)

POZZO: Faster! (*He crosses the stage preceded by Lucky. Vladimir and Estragon take off their hats, wave their hands. Exit Lucky. Pozzo cracks rope and whip.*) On! On! (*On the point of disappearing in his turn he stops and turns. The rope tautens. Noise of Lucky falling off.*) Stool! (*Vladimir fetches stool and gives it to Pozzo who throws it to Lucky.*) Adieu!

VLADIMIR AND ESTRAGON: (*waving*) Adieu! Adieu!

POZZO: Up! Pig! (*Noise of Lucky getting up.*) On! (*Exit Pozzo. Crack of whip.*) Faster! On! Adieu! Pig! Yip! Adieu!

(*Long silence.*)

VLADIMIR: That passed the time.

ESTRAGON: It would have passed in any case.

VLADIMIR: Yes, but not so rapidly. (*Pause.*)

ESTRAGON: What do we do now?

VLADIMIR: I don't know.

ESTRAGON: Let's go.

VLADIMIR: We can't.

ESTRAGON: Why not?

VLADIMIR: We're waiting for Godot.

ESTRAGON: Ah! (*Pause.*)

VLADIMIR: How they've changed!

ESTRAGON: Who?

VLADIMIR: Those two.

ESTRAGON: That's the idea. Let's make a little conversation.

VLADIMIR: Haven't they?

ESTRAGON: What?

VLADIMIR: Changed.

ESTRAGON: Very likely. They all change. Only we can't.

VLADIMIR: Likely! It's certain. Didn't you see them?

ESTRAGON: I suppose I did. But I don't know them.

VLADIMIR: Yes you do know them.

ESTRAGON: No I don't know them.

VLADIMIR: We know them, I tell you. You forget everything. (*Pauses. To himself.*) Unless they're not the same . . .

ESTRAGON: Why didn't they recognize us then?

VLADIMIR: That means nothing. I too pretended not to recognize them. And then nobody ever recognizes us.

ESTRAGON: Forget it. What we need—Ow! (*He holds his foot. Vladimir pays no attention.*) Ow!

VLADIMIR: (*To himself.*) Unless they're not the same . . .

ESTRAGON: Didi! It's the other foot! (*He hobbles.*)

VLADIMIR: Unless they're not the same . . .

BOY: (*Off stage*) Mister! (*They both look towards the voice.*)

ESTRAGON: Off we go again.

VLADIMIR: Approach, my child.

(*Enter Boy, timidly. He halts.*)

BOY: Mister Albert . . . ?

VLADIMIR: Yes.

ESTRAGON: What do you want?

VLADIMIR: Approach. (*The Boy does not move.*)

ESTRAGON: (*forcibly*) Approach when you're told, can't you? (*The Boy advances timidly. Halts.*)

VLADIMIR: What is it?

BOY: Mr. Godot . . .

VLADIMIR: Obviously. (*Pause.*) Approach. (*The boy does not move.*)

ESTRAGON: (*violently*) Will you approach! (*The boy advances timidly, halts.*) What kept you so late?

VLADIMIR: You have a message from Mr. Godot?

BOY: Yes sir.

VLADIMIR: Well, what is it?

ESTRAGON: What kept you so late?

(*The Boy looks at them in turn, not knowing to which he should reply.*)

VLADIMIR: (*to Estragon*) Let him alone.

ESTRAGON: You let me alone. (*Advancing to the Boy.*) Do you know what time it is?

BOY: (*recoiling*) It's not my fault, sir.

ESTRAGON: And whose is it? Mine?

BOY: I was afraid, sir.

ESTRAGON: Afraid of what? Of us? (*Pause.*) Answer me!

VLADIMIR: I know what it is, he was afraid of the others.

ESTRAGON: How long have you been here?

BOY: A good while, sir.

VLADIMIR: You were afraid of the whip.

BOY: Yes, sir.

VLADIMIR: The roars.

BOY: Yes, sir.

VLADIMIR: The two big men.

BOY: Yes, sir.

VLADIMIR: Do you know them?

BOY: No, sir.

VLADIMIR: Are you a native of these parts? (*Silence.*) Do you belong to these parts?

BOY: Yes, sir.

ESTRAGON: That's all a pack of lies. (*Shaking the Boy by the arm.*) Tell us the truth.

BOY: (*trembling*) But it is the truth, sir!

VLADIMIR: Will you let him alone! What's the matter with you? (*Estragon releases the Boy, moves away, covering his face with his hands. Vladimir and the Boy watch him. Estragon drops his hands. His face is convulsed.*) What's the matter with you?

ESTRAGON: I'm unhappy.

VLADIMIR: Not really! Since when?

ESTRAGON: I'd forgotten.

VLADIMIR: Extraordinary the tricks that memory plays! (*Estragon tries to speak, renounces, limps to a mound, sits down and begins to take off his boot. Vladimir turns to the Boy.*) Well?

BOY: Mr. Godot—

VLADIMIR: I've seen you before, haven't I?

BOY: I don't know, sir.

VLADIMIR: You don't know me?

BOY: No, sir.

VLADIMIR: It wasn't you came yesterday?

BOY: No, sir.

VLADIMIR: This is your first time?

BOY: Yes, sir. (*Silence.*)

VLADIMIR: Words, words. (*Pause.*) Speak.

BOY: (*In a rush*) Mr. Godot told me to tell you he won't come this evening but surely tomorrow. (*Silence.*)

VLADIMIR: Is that all?

BOY: Yes, sir.

VLADIMIR: You work for Mr. Godot?

BOY: Yes, sir.

VLADIMIR: What do you do?

BOY: I mind the goats, sir.

VLADIMIR: Is he good to you?

BOY: Yes, sir.

VLADIMIR: He doesn't beat you?

BOY: No, sir, not me.

VLADIMIR: Whom does he beat?

BOY: He beats my brother, sir.

VLADIMIR: Ah, you have a brother?

BOY: Yes, sir.

VLADIMIR: What does he do?

BOY: He minds the sheep, sir.

VLADIMIR: And why doesn't he beat you?

BOY: I don't know, sir.

VLADIMIR: He must be fond of you.

BOY: I don't know, sir.

VLADIMIR: Does he give you enough to eat? (*The Boy hesitates*) Does he feed you well?

BOY: Fairly well, sir.

VLADIMIR: You're not unhappy? (*The Boy hesitates*.) Do you hear me?

BOY: Yes, sir.

VLADIMIR: Well?

BOY: I don't know, sir.

VLADIMIR: You don't know if you're unhappy or not?

BOY: No, sir.

VLADIMIR: You're like myself. (*Pause*.) Where do you sleep?

BOY: In the loft, sir.

VLADIMIR: With your brother?

BOY: Yes, sir.

VLADIMIR: In the hay?

BOY: Yes, sir. (*Silence*.)

VLADIMIR: All right, you may go.

BOY: What am I to say to Mr. Godot, sir?

VLADIMIR: Tell him . . . (*he hesitates*) . . . tell him you saw us. (*Pause*.) You did see us, didn't you?

BOY: Yes, sir.

(*He steps back, hesitates, turns and exits running. The light fails suddenly. In a moment it is night. The moon rises at back, mounts in the sky, stands still, shedding a pale light on the scene.*)

VLADIMIR: At last! (*Estragon gets up and goes towards Vladimir,*

a boot in each hand. He puts them down at the edge of the stage,
straightens and contemplates the moon.) What are you doing?

ESTRAGON: Pale for weariness.

VLADIMIR: Eh?

ESTRAGON: Of climbing heaven and gazing on the likes of us.

VLADIMIR: Your boots. What are you doing with your boots?

ESTRAGON: (*turning to look at his boots.*) I'm leaving them there.
(*Pause.*) Another will come, just as . . . as . . . as me, but with
smaller feet, and they'll make him happy.

VLADIMIR: But you can't go barefoot!

ESTRAGON: Christ did.

VLADIMIR: Christ! What's Christ got to do with it? You're
not going to compare yourself to Christ?

ESTRAGON: All my life I've compared myself to Him.

VLADIMIR: But where He was it was warm, it was dry!

ESTRAGON: Yes, and they crucified quick. (*Silence.*)

VLADIMIR: We've nothing more to do here.

ESTRAGON: Nor anywhere else.

VLADIMIR: Ah, Gogo, don't go on like that. Tomorrow everything will be better.

ESTRAGON: How do you make that out?

VLADIMIR: Did you not hear what the child said?

ESTRAGON: No.

VLADIMIR: He said that Godot was sure to come tomorrow.
(*Pause.*) What do you say to that?

ESTRAGON: Then all we have to do is to wait on here.

VLADIMIR: Are you mad? We must take cover. (*He takes
Estragon by the arm.*) Come on. (*He draws Estragon after him.
Estragon yields, then resists. They halt.*)

ESTRAGON: (*Looking at the tree.*) Pity we haven't got a bit of
rope.

VLADIMIR: Come on. It's getting cold. (*He draws him after him.
As before.*)

ESTRAGON: Remind me to bring a bit of rope tomorrow.

VLADIMIR: Yes, yes. Come on. (*He draws him after him. As
before.*)

ESTRAGON: How long have we been together all the time now?

VLADIMIR: I don't know. Fifty years perhaps.

ESTRAGON: Do you remember the day I threw myself into the
Rhône?

VLADIMIR: We were grape-harvesting.

ESTRAGON: You fished me out.

VLADIMIR: That's all dead and buried.

ESTRAGON: My clothes dried in the sun.

VLADIMIR: There's no use harking back on that. Come on. (*He draws him after him. As before.*)

ESTRAGON: Wait.

VLADIMIR: I'm cold.

ESTRAGON: Wait! (*He moves away from Vladimir.*) I wonder if we wouldn't have been better off alone, each one for himself. (*He crosses the stage and sits down on a mound.*) We weren't made for the same road.

VLADIMIR: (*without anger*) It's not certain.

ESTRAGON: No, nothing is certain.

(*Vladimir slowly crosses the stage and sits down beside Estragon.*)

VLADIMIR: We can still part, if you think it would be better.

ESTRAGON: It's too late now.

(*Silence.*)

VLADIMIR: Yes, it's too late now.

(*Silence.*)

ESTRAGON: Well, shall we go?

VLADIMIR: Yes, let's go.

(*They do not move.*)

           (*Curtain.*)